Kursmodell Englisch

Shakespeare's MACBETH

Karl Emunds

Langenscheidt-Longman
ENGLISH LANGUAGE TEACHING

Kursmodell Englisch
Shakespeare's MACBETH

Erarbeitet von
StD Dr. Karl Emunds, Aachen

unter beratender Mitwirkung von
Prof. Dr. Wilfried Brusch, Hamburg
Anthony Laude, M. A., London
Gerald Nixon, B. A., Berlin

Verlagsredaktion Langenscheidt-Longman
Eva Hochrath, M. A.; Dr. Siegfried Birle

Umschlag: Christel Langer, München
Graphik: ZERO – Angewandte Grafik, München

1. Auflage 1983

Druck: Druckhaus Langenscheidt, Berlin-Schöneberg
Printed in Germany: 3-526-50325-8

3 4 5 6 7 * 91 90 89 88 87

CONTENTS

Part II: Close Reading of the Play

Part III: Beyond the Text: Topics for discussion

Part IV: Reception of the Play

Abbreviations

BE	British English
cf.	compare
1 d	1 (old) penny
E	English
eds.	editors
e.g.	for example
et al.	and other writers, authors, etc.
f./ff.	and the following line(s) or page(s)
F	French
i.e.	that is
inf.	infinitive
L	Latin
l./ll.	line(s)
o.s.	oneself
p./pp.	page(s)
repr.	reprinted
rev.	revised
1 s.	1 shilling
$ 1	1 dollar
s.o.	someone
s.th.	something
vol./vols.	volume(s)

Symbols

★	scene/unit that is essential
☆	scene/unit that can be omitted
●●	it is strongly recommended that this question be answered
●	it is recommended that this question be answered
○	question which may be omitted if time is limited, etc.
➧	look up this term in the "Glossary of Literary Terms"
Ⓖ	question the different parts of which can be assigned to different groups

Introduction

Who is afraid of William Shakespeare? Should you have any doubts about difficulties you might have when reading one of his plays you can make use of this Students' Book on MACBETH. It offers a closer look at Shakespeare's life, the story of his stage, the printing of his plays, the conditions of his age, and some details about MACBETH, with regard to its sources, its text and the date of its first performance **(Part I: Background Reading).** Not all the background texts need be read. The contents of some of them may be summarized and reported in class. A good knowledge of these texts, however, will help you to appreciate MACBETH more easily and to understand its basic ideas more fully.

When reading MACBETH you may proceed from scene to scene, following each single unit in **Part II: Close Reading of the Play.** The scenes which are marked by ☆ can be omitted. You may even decide to concentrate only on those scenes which are marked by ★. In these cases you will save time at the expense of a complete understanding of the play although synopses of the omitted scenes may be given in the classroom.

Each scene of the Close Reading of the Text in Part II is introduced by some keyword(s) pointing out its function in the play (i.e. Exposition, Rising Action, etc.) and by a quotation taken from the text, signalling the most important aspect from which the scene may be regarded. The **Phrases for discussing the scene** will help you to express your thoughts more easily when discussing the scene. Especially phrases which are in bold type should be learnt.

It is intended to be flexible, both for teachers, who may have to work with groups of different achievement levels, and for students, whose interest and motivation may vary. Therefore the questions under **Comprehension** and **Analysis** are either marked as strongly recommended (●●) and as recommended (●) or left unmarked or even qualified as questions which may be omitted if time is limited (○).

In the **Comprehension questions** you may be asked to paraphrase some of the more important passages with the help of your notes in the *New Swan Shakespeare* text (see the last paragraph of this Introduction) or to give a plot synopsis. Most of the questions are aimed at making sure that you have understood the main events and essential details given in a particular scene. They may also require you to structure a text and give your reasons for doing so.

Questions under **Analysis** are intended to guide you to a closer interpretation of a single scene, asking you to concentrate on various aspects such as setting, characterization, plot, atmosphere, dialogue, style and structure of the play or on items of historical or political interest. Questions under **Text Production** are meant to invite you to discuss an interesting or controversial topic of a scene either by preparing notes for a short talk in the classroom or by writing a short essay on the subject.

When you have finished your close reading of MACBETH you are offered a choice of four different approaches to the play, each of them providing the possibility of one final synthesis **(Part III: Beyound the Text).** You need not take all of them, as it is sufficient to concentrate on one or two single aspects which may be of particular interest.

You can also try to study the problem of how one of the most important passages of the play has been translated into German **(Part IV: Reception of the Play 1: A note on translations).** If you compare three different translations you will recognize the different aims and methods of the translators and the resulting shortcomings and advantages of their German version of the text. **In Reception 2: A note of performances** you are given an example of how stage directors of different countries and different decades staged MACBETH as they saw it: a passage taken from M. Rosenberg's book *The Masks of Macbeth,* Berkeley, 1978, serves to illustrate how four lines of the play were differently rendered by famous actresses to impersonate Lady Macbeth in Act I, Scene 3.

The **Glossary of Literary Terms** (Part V) offers you the possibility of looking up terms you may need when analysing or evaluating the play or some of its elements. References to such terms are indicated by this sign: ➧. The terms listed will also be of use for you when analysing a modern English or American drama.

The standard reference text used in this students' Book is the *New Swan Shakespeare MACBETH*, edited by Bernard Lott, M.A., London 1977, 3rd edition, reprinted.

Karl Emunds January, 1983

The phonetic transcription used in this book is based on the Jones/Gimson-standard as realized in *the Dictionary of Contemporary English,* Langenscheidt-Longman, Munich.

Caithness
NORTH
SEA
Moray Firth
Ross&Cromarty
HIGH-
Forres
Macduff
Cawdor
Inverness
LANDS
Lochaber
Angus
Birnam
Glamis
Dunsinane
Colme-Kill
Bertha Castle
Scone
Firth of Tay
Perth
Fife
Menteith
Kingcorn
Culross
St.Colme's Inch
Firth of Forth
Edinburgh
SOUTHERN
UPLANDS
Northumberland
Cumberland

Part I: Background Reading

1. Shakespeare and his audience

1.1. Shakespeare's life

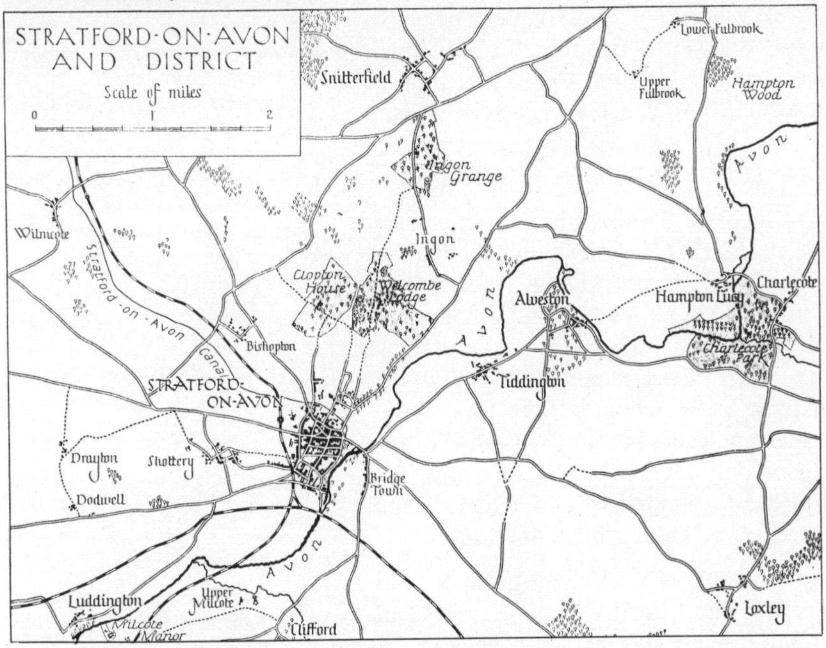

Based upon the Ordnance Survey Map with the sanction of the Controller of H. M. Stationery Office

The Holy Trinity Church

William Shakespeare was born in the prosperous market-town of Stratford-on-Avon, Warwickshire. His christening was registered on 26 April 1564, probably three days after his birth. William's parents were Mary Arden, who came from an old and respected family of local landowners, and John Shakespeare, a prominent citizen and a well-to-do glover and dealer in agricultural products, particularly wool and hides. They had eight children. William was their third child and eldest son. He probably attended the local grammar school where he would have received a fairly good education. We don't know whether he was able to complete his course of education there, because his father, who had taken a leading part in the administration of Stratford and who had held several public offices in the town till at last he rose to the office of bailiff, the equivalent of the mayor in those days, suddenly withdrew from public life. As John Shakespeare mortgaged part of his wife's property in 1577 it is probable that he had run into financial difficulties. He never became poor, however, for he never sold his double house in Henley Street.

→ **Warwickshire** ['wɒrɪkʃə] country in central England
→ **christening** ['krɪsənɪŋ] ceremony of receiving s.o. (usually a small child) into the Christian Church and of giving him or her a name
→ **glover** ['glʌvə^{r}] maker or supplier of gloves (Handschuhe)
→ **to mortgage** ['mɔːgɪdʒ] to give s.o. the right or a claim to the ownership of (a house, land, etc.) in return for money lent for a certain period

At the age of eighteen William Shakespeare married Ann Hathaway, who was about eight years older than himself. She was the daughter of a farmer who owned land in Shottery, a village near Stratford. In 1583, five months after the date of their marriage licence, their daughter Susan was born. There may not have been any disgrace about this, for in respectable Elizabethan families the actual marriage often took place months before the church ceremony for which the licence was issued: in such cases the church wedding was considered as a kind of after-ceremony. In 1585 the twins Hamnet and Judith were born.

The next period in Shakespeare's life is a blank – the so-called "lost years". There is no documentary evidence of where he was living and what he was doing during this period. It is not known when he left Stratford and went to London, but by 1594 he must have become quite successful as an actor and a writer of plays, narrative poems, and sonnets, for he was already arousing interest in court circles and feelings of ill-will among some of his fellow-dramatists. Some scholars think that Shakespeare's career as a dramatist began some years before 1590, while others suppose that he began writing plays only after 1590. At any rate, it is known for certain that by 1592 he was a playwright and actor of some fame, though we do not know where he had been trained as an actor.

In 1594 William Shakespeare was a member of a newly re-grouped company of actors who called themselves the "Lord Chamberlain's Company" and who at first performed their plays at the "Theatre" at Shoreditch on the north bank of the River Thames. The Theatre, which had been erected by James Burbage in 1576, was the first English playhouse to be specially built for the performance of plays. It had been built outside the boundaries of the City of London as the authorities had objected to play-acting within the City walls. They were obviously afraid of further outbreaks of the plague, which had been a serious problem in 1592 and 1593 and which could spread rapidly wherever people were gathered together. They also disliked private performances in inn yards, or in the halls of noblemen's houses, or in any public place where a stage could be erected as they were afraid of the disorder that might be caused by noisy crowds and could not tolerate any witty criticism of prominent people by playwrights or actors. As the actors themselves belonged to a profession which had not yet won social acceptance, they sought the protection of powerful noblemen who acted as their patrons, supporting them as members of their households, and helped them to obtain licenses to perform their plays. Thus Shakespeare's company, the Chamberlain's Men as they were also called, were under the protection of the Lord Chamberlain, an official of the royal household who was responsible not only for the royal palaces and the royal wardrobe but also for all entertainments given before the Queen and her Court. His protection was particularly important to Shakespeare and his fellow actors as the Lord Chamberlain could give orders to the Master of the Revels, an official of his department who arranged, supervised and paid for all kinds of court entertainments. The Master of the Revels also had the right to read and to give official approval for all plays before they were staged or even printed. Thus the Master of the Revels could censor any play.

→ **a blank** empty space; (here:) an unknown period in Shakespeare's life
→ **narrative** ['nærətɪv] telling a story or having the form of a story
→ **sonnet** fourteen-line poem with a formal pattern of rhymes
→ **playwright** ['pleɪraɪt] writer of plays
→ **plague** [pleɪg] disease that spreads very quickly, producing high fever and causing rapid death
→ **patron** ['peɪtrən] high-placed person who gives support or encouragement to s.o.

Besides the Lord Chamberlain's Men and other acting companies under the protection of persons of influence there was a group of players which had been founded under the patronage of the Lord Admiral a few weeks before: the Lord Admiral's Men. They performed their plays at the Rose Theatre, which had been opened by its manager Philip Henslowe in 1592 on the south bank of the river, on the Bankside in Southwark.

The Lord Chamberlain's Company, which Shakespeare joined in 1594, included James Burbage's son Richard Burbage and John Heminge and Henry Condell, who later published the First Folio edition of Shakespeare's plays. Richard Burbage's brother Cuthbert also seems to have been connected with the company, although he was no actor himself. It was men like Heminge and Condell who, together with Shakespeare himself, acted the famous plays Shakespeare was to write for them. Shakespeare was to remain with this company as one of its leading actors and shareholders until he retired in about 1611.

When in 1598 the lease of the land on which the Theatre stood had almost expired the chief shareholders of the company decided to save their property, which otherwise would have been claimed by the owner of the land. So they pulled down the Theatre and used the timber to build the Globe Theatre on a site which they had already bought. The company probably moved to the new theatre in 1599. The Globe was situated just across London Bridge, on the Bankside, quite close to the Rose. Shakespeare was one of the chief shareholders of the company who had invested some of their capital in the Globe. "In the case of the Globe, half the ownership was given to Cuthbert and Richard Burbage, the latter the leading actor of the company, and the other half was divided equally among five actor-sharers, including Shakespeare".[1] As an actor of the company Shakespeare took a share of the entrance money. Together with Shakespeare's and his fellow actors' talents this effective organization contributed to the success of the Lord Chamberlain's Company. Till it burned down in 1613 the Globe was famous as the theatre where Shakespeare's plays were performed and attracted not only the craftsmen and shopkeepers of London but also the fashionable and aristocratic circles of the City and the court. The Chamberlain's Men, who became the King's Men after King James's accession to the throne in 1603, were the most famous company of actors in London. Undoubtedly Shakespeare himself largely contributed to this fame, for almost every year he wrote two plays which were added to the repertory of the company. "What it is equally important to keep in mind, however, is that Shakespeare without the Chamberlain's Men would have been a lesser Shakespeare. At a time when most playwrights were living a hand-to-mouth existence as free-lance writers, Shakespeare enjoyed the advantages of a permanent and prominent position with a group of experienced and talented actors with whose limitations and capacities he could become intimately acquainted. Added to this is the evidence that the members were friends as well as colleagues, that they were, throughout most of their careers, free of the economic oppression of theatre owners like Philip Henslowe and, finally, that membership in the company was extraordinarily stable during most of Shakespeare's career."[2] Shake-

→ **patronage** ['peɪtrənɪdʒ] support, encouragement given by a patron
→ **shareholder** an owner of one or more shares (the equal parts into which the capital of a company is divided; the shareholder has the right to claim a proportion of the profits of the company)
→ **lease** contract by which a person pays money (usually a rent) to use land, buildings, etc. which he does not own
→ **to expire** (of a period of time, or a lease) to come to an end
→ **repertory** ['repətəri] collection of plays, pieces of music, etc. that a performer or a theatre company has learnt and can perform
→ **lesser** less great
→ **free-lance** independent; not working just for one employer

speare's growing success as a playwright and a shareholder enabled him to make considerable purchases of land in Stratford during the twenty years he was in London. For his family he acquired New Place, one of the finest houses in Stratford. He was to retire there when he left London in about 1611.

In 1608 the King's Men bought a more comfortable and expensive theatre within the City walls. It was a former Blackfriars' monastery a part of which had been converted into a roofed theatre where a company of boy actors, the "Children of Blackfriars", had performed their plays. The King's Men used Blackfriars as an indoor theatre for performing plays during the winter months. They were no longer obliged to use the open-air Globe Theatre in winter, although performances there did not come to an end. As a result takings were considerably increased.

In order to appeal to the smaller and more refined audience at Blackfriars they began putting on plays that were different in style and content from those they had presented before: romances, stories of love, adventure and strange events set in long-past periods of faraway places – plays whose endings were happier than real life. It may seem surprising that during Shakespeare's lifetime the King's Men no longer met with any strong opposition to their acting plays at Blackfriars when influential people must have lived in the neighbourhood. Probably the company had become so popular and was in so high official favour that the City authorities offered no further resistance to the actors and their plays.

In 1610 and 1611, when he was writing his last comedies, Shakespeare seems to have been living in Stratford. One event may be regarded as the symbolic end of his life as an actor and a dramatist: On 2 July 1613 the Globe burnt down during a performance of HENRY VIII when the thatched roof of the galleries caught fire. Shakespeare apparently spent his last few years quietly in his native town. He died there on 23 April 1616. The cause of his death is not known. He was buried at the eastern end of Holy Trinity Church at Stratford.

William Shakespeare actor and playwright

There is a monument to him by the London sculptor Gheerart Janssen, which was probably put up within seven years of his death. Janssen's bust is regarded as one of the few existing life-like representations of Shakespeare's features. Ben Jonson, who both admired and criticized the great poet, is supposed to have written the epitaph on Shakespeare's gravestone in Holy Trinity Church. Some scholars, however, maintain that Shakespare himself devised this epitaph:

→ **Blackfriars** ['blækfraɪəz] a district of London just north of the river (so named because in the 13th century the religious order of the Dominicans or "Black Friars" built a large convent there)
→ **thatched** made of straw
→ **Trinity** (in the Christian religion) the union of the three forms of God (Father, Son and Holy Spirit)
→ **bust** human head, shoulders and chest, as represented by the art of the sculptor (Bildhauer)
→ **epitaph** ['epɨta:f] short description of a dead person, often written on a stone over his or her grave
→ **to devise** to invent
→ **forbear to dig** do not dig
→ **blest** (poetic for "blessed") fortunate; having God on one's side
→ **curst** (poetic for "cursed") unfortunate, damned; having God against one.

("Good friend, for Jesus' sake forbear
To dig the dust enclosed here!
Blest be the man that spares these stones,
An curst be he that moves my bones.")

> GOOD FREND FOR IESVS SAKE FORBEARE,
> TO DIGG THE DVST ENCLOASED HEARE!
> BLESTE BE Y^{E} MAN Y^{T} SPARES THES STONES,
> AND CURST BE HE Y^{T} MOVES MY BONES.

1 Joan Cenedella. "Shakespeare, William (1564–1616)", in *A Shakespeare Encyclopaedia,* ed. Oscar James Campbell, Edward G. Quinn. London: Methuen, 1966, p. 765.
2 Edward Quinn, "Chamberlain's Men (1594–1603) [(Lord Hudson's Men (1596–1597), King's Men (1603–1642)]", in Campbell/Quinn, p. 101.

1.2. London, its people and audiences

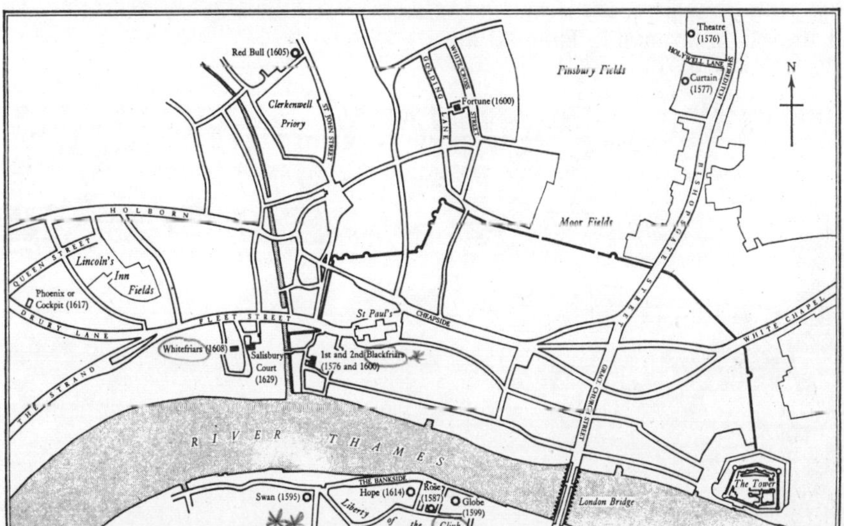

A map of the London playhouses. Based on a drawing in J. Q. Adams, Shakespearean Playhouses (London 1920), frontispiece.

In Shakespeare's time London was already a place of great political and economic importance with a large population. For about 500 years the royal court with its law courts and administrative offices had had its seat at Westminster, making it a centre of diplomatic life and administrative decision-making. The two Houses of Parliament also met there for their financial debates.

The city of London had long before achieved a degree of self-government and some independence of the Crown, and had also become (along with Oxford and Cambridge) one of the main centres of English intellectual life.

The City was a major centre for both inland and overseas trade, which expanded considerably as the great English navigators and sailors went in search of new sea-routes and explored the far-away countries of the New World and chartered companies for trade with Russia, the Near East, and East India were founded. The Royal Exchange, established by Queen Elizabeth for merchants to meet and do business together, was later replaced by the Stock Exchange, a kind of market where members bought and sold the shares of the joint-stock overseas trading companies. Thus the rich merchants of the City helped to pay for the expeditions of the pioneers and adventurers who sailed unknown seas and explored distant countries to open up new markets for England.

Ever since the 12th century Italian money-lenders had lived in Lombard Street, and in Shakespeare's days this was London's principal banking and money-changing centre. It was here that bills of exchange to finance trading both at home and overseas were issued and sold. Apart from the merchants, shopkeepers and the students who crowded London's streets there were also all the craftsmen, labourers, carriers, servants, and apprentices who lived and worked within the City walls. Nor should we forget the courtiers, lawyers, officers, fashionable women, ordinary housewives and children, or the seamen ashore, the dismissed soldiers, the peddlers, the thieves, and the "light women". They all must have made a colourful picture.

→ **chartered** having been given special rights by the Crown
→ **stock exchange** place where the shares of a company (stock) are bought and sold
→ **joint-stock company** company owned by all the people who have bought shares in it
→ **bill of exchange** a written order to pay money on a certain date
→ **peddler** (often BE pedlar) person who goes from place to place selling small articles

THE SOUTH BANK OF THE THAMES, showing the Globe Theatre and a bear-garden, from Hollar's View of London, 1647

Together with visits to bull- and bear-baiting arenas, cockpits (where cockfights took place) and taverns, theatre-going was one of the favourite pastimes of almost all the groups we have just listed. For many of them the Elizabethan "public" and "private" theatres or the inn-yards where plays were often performed were within easy walking distance. On some days there was a choice of plays to go and see, for those who could afford it. People such as those mentioned above formed the mixed audiences of the "public" theatres which "catered for all comers, primarily for the crowd who stood in the open around the stage, and only secondarily for the wealthier patrons who sat at a distance in the seclusion of the surrounding galleries or lords' rooms. The so-called 'private' playhouses, on the other hand, were located to begin with in the halls of existing buildings. They had benches next to the stage, where the wealthy sat, as well as galleries, a much smaller audience capacity, and much higher admission prices".[3]

According to Alfred Harbage "we should distinguish among three Elizabethan audiences . . . : there was the genteel audience of the private theatres; there was the plebeian audience of such theatres as the Red Bull and perhaps the Fortune after the private houses had filched the gentry away; and then there was that audience both genteel and plebeian, or neither, of the nineties and, because of its peculiar prestige, of the Globe in the early decades of the seventeenth century. It was the audience for which nearly all the great Elizabethan plays were written. It was Shakespeare's audience.

"All that we can say of the composition of Shakespeare's audience, other than that it was a cross section of the London population of his day, is that youth may have predominated somewhat over age, male over female, the worldly over the pious, and, of course without the 'perhaps' the receptive over the unreceptive. Although the more leisured classes would have been better represented than by their pro rata of the population, it was predominantly a working-class audience because of the great numerical superiority of the working classes in the London area and because theatrical tariffs had been designed largely for them."[4]

→ **bull-baiting; bear-baiting** sport (popular in Elizabethan England) of setting dogs to attack bulls or bears, which were chained to a post
→ **tavern** ['tævən] (old word for) inn: pub, public house where drinks are served
→ **to cater for** (here) to offer plays suitable for
→ **patron** ['peɪtrən] paying member of the audience
→ **seclusion** privacy, separateness
→ **genteel** [dʒen'tiːl] of high social class
→ **plebeian** [plɪ'biːən] of low social class
→ **to filch** [fɪltʃ] to take, steal
→ **cross section** group that is representative (of the whole population)
→ **to predominate** to be more numerous than
→ **the worldly** people who are more attracted to the pleasures of this world than concerned with the next
→ **the pious** ['paɪəs] very religious people
→ **the receptive** [rɪ'septɪv] people interested in new ideas and experiences
→ **leisured** ['leʒəd] having plenty of free time
→ **pro rata** [ˌprəʊ'raːtə] (here) percentage
→ **numerical superiority** being present in great numbers

3 Andrew Gurr, *The Elizabethan Stage 1574–1642.* Cambridge: University Press, 1970, p. 82.

4 Alfred Harbage. *Shakespeare's Audience.* New York and London: Columbia University Press, Columbia Paperback Edition, 1969, 3rd edition, repr., p. 90.

2. Macbeth: from a historical person to a literary figure

2.1. The historical Macbeth

Some years after the two separate Scottish kingdoms of the Picts and Scots were united in the 9th century, there were two Scottish royal lines. Now the right to kingship no longer passed alternately from brother to brother or from uncle to nephew of one royal line. Instead, it went from the eldest member of one branch to the senior leader of the other. When in the 11th century the crown was claimed by three different royal lines, the question of succession, which had never been easy to settle, increasingly became a matter of violent dispute. Between the middle of the 10th and the end of the 11th century as many as twelve Scottish kings were killed in feuds or murdered by their successors.

→ **kingship** office of king, or quality of being king
→ **alternately** [ɔ:l'tɜ:nətli] (of two things) one after the other
→ **to claim** to demand (as a right)
→ **feud** [fju:d] conflict, usually between two rivals or rival families

The historical Macbeth is apparently no exception to the rule. He was the son of the provincial ruler of Moray and Ross, who had been murdered by his nephews. When one of his father's murderers died in 1029, he became governor of this region whose independence of the crown had grown during the previous centuries. Historians say that Macbeth may have had a double claim to the Scottish throne; both his mother and his wife were apparently members of royal houses. However true this may be, it is a historical fact that Macbeth, in order to succeed to the throne, killed his cousin, King Duncan, and was in turn killed by Duncan's son Malcolm.

His comparatively long rule – seventeen years – seems to indicate that he was a strong king. The historical Macbeth appears to have been a good ruler who was generous to the church and who brought prosperity to his country. Even so, there were several attempts to overthrow his rule but only the one led by Duncan's son Malcolm in 1057 was successful. Together with Siward, Earl of Northumbria and a relation of his, Malcolm invaded Scotland; after a long and hard fight he defeated and killed Macbeth, thus establishing his rule over the whole of the united kingdom of the Picts and the Scots north of the Forth-Clyde line.

2.2. Some of Shakespeare's sources

The sixteenth century was a century of renewed literary activity. The invention in England of the printing press by William Caxton in 1471 and the new spirit of learning which characterized the Renaissance encouraged more and more people to write down their knowledge of a particular subject so that it could be imparted to a greater number of people. Thus, by the time Shakespeare started to write MACBETH in the early years of the seventeenth century, there was already quite a considerable number of books from which he could have drawn his information not only about the historical events surrounding Macbeth's murder of Duncan but also about such themes as witchcraft and demonology or kingship and tyranny.

Shakespeare's choice of the historical figure of Macbeth as a subject for a play seems to be associated with the new king of England. When Elizabeth I died without children in 1603, the reigning king of Scotland, James VI, became James I of England. It was common belief at that time that James was a descendant of Banquo and MACBETH is not the only play of that period to deal with Banquo's fate. On the King's visit to Oxford in 1605 a play entitled "Tres Sibyllae" by M. Gwinn was performed for his benefit. In it, three 'sibyls', women who were able to foretell the future, prophesied an empire without end to Banquo and the following generations of his family. It is not known whether Shakespeare knew of this play when he wrote MACBETH, but it is likely that he knew about the King's interest in witchcraft. The King himself had written a book in 1597 which he called "Daemonologie" and in which witches were said to be able to predict the outcome of battles and foretell the future of kingdoms. Among other books on witchcraft, such as Reginald Scott's "Discoveries of Witchcraft" (1584) in which the author criticized the belief in witchcraft and wrote in defence of poor, elderly or simple persons who were believed to be witches, there is one in particular which has close parallels to at least one of the motifs of MACBETH. Shakespeare may also have known of the report on a witch trial the king was involved in, given in the "News from Scotland of Doctor Fian a Notable Sorcerer" (1591). In 1605 a translation of de Loier's book, in English "Treatise of Specters", was printed in which the murdered victims of kings appeared to them later, especially at meal times.

The King's other great interest was statecraft and he wrote at least two books on this subject which contain themes which are echoed in MACBETH. In "Basilikon Doron" (1599) King James contrasts the qualities of a good king with those of a tyrant, and in "A Counterblaste to Tobacco" (1604) a king is regarded as a physician to his country. In Act IV, Scene 3 of MACBETH Malcolm takes up both these motifs in his testing of Macduff.

It would not have been difficult for Shakespeare to gather information on the historical Macbeth. In the 16th century at least four histories of Scotland were printed which dealt with the lives of Macbeth and Banquo at some length and which contain details to be found in Shakespeare's drama. The first of these was Hector Boece's "Scotorum Historiae", printed in 1527, which speaks of Lady Macbeth's intense desire to become queen, her criticism of her husband and her doubts about his manhood. In Leslie's "De Origine, Moribus, et Rebus Gestis Scotorum" (1578) it is told how Macbeth overheard the prophesy given to Banquo about his descendants by three devils disguised as women; also mentioned is Lady Macbeth's victory over her husband's scruples. In "Rerum Scotorum Historia" (1582) Buchanan's account of Macbeth's character is very close to Shakespeare's own: ambitious and cruel, Macbeth becomes a tyrant and cannot suppress his feelings of guilt about Duncan's murder; he is tormented by visions of horror which prevent him from sleeping and is addressed by a voice from heaven; he regards Banquo as a rival and threat to his ambitions and lives in fear of him.

→ **to renew** to begin again
→ **particular** special
→ **to impart** to pass on to s.o. else (information, a secret, etc.)
→ **witchcraft** techniques, practices and rituals of witches
→ **demonology** [ˌdiːməˈnɒlədʒɪ] study of demons [iː] and evil spirits
→ **for s.o.'s benefit** specially for s.o.
→ **to predict** to already know and say what will happen in future
→ **outcome** result, end
→ **statecraft** art of managing the affairs of a country
→ **physician** [fɪˈzɪʃən] doctor
→ **to disguise** to dress up in order to hide one's identity

Shakespeare's chief source, however, were the "Chronicles of England, Scotlande, and Irelande" by Raphael Holinshed, first printed in 1577 but enlarged and published in a second edition ten years later. Although the "Chronicles" were largely an uncritical compilation of texts from many different sources (he copied and supplemented Wyntoun's "Orygnale Cronykil of Scotland" (c. 1424); the section on Scotland was mainly a translation of Boece's "Scotorum Historiae";) they were extremely popular in Shakespeare's time and provided many Elizabethan dramatists with subjects for their plays. Shakespeare was no exception and based not only many of his historical plays but also some of his tragedies and romantic plays on material he found there. Macbeth, Lear and Cymbeline are only three examples of British kings whom Shakespeare made the subject of dramas after reading about their lives in Holinshed's "Chronicles".

For both political and dramatic reasons, Shakespeare was obliged to alter some of the basic facts recorded by Holinshed. For example, Holinshed's young and weak ruler King Duncan becomes a gentle, almost saintlike, old man in Shakespeare's play. According to Holinshed, Duncan rejects Macbeth's legal claim to the throne and names his son Malcolm Prince of Cumberland and his successor; Shakespeare makes no mention of Macbeth's legal claim to the Scottish throne. Again, Banquo is portrayed by Shakespeare as an honest and loyal subject of the king (it must be remembered that he was one of King James's ancestors); Holinshed writes that Banquo belonged to the group of conspirators around Macbeth who were responsible for the murder of Duncan. Finally, Shakespeare has shortened Holinshed's account of the campaigns of the Scottish armies. The single battle described by the messenger in the first scenes of the play, which serves to introduce Macbeth to the audience, is in fact a combination of three different battles in which Macbeth was victorious and in which he earned his reputation as a courageous and bold warrior.

At the same time, Shakespeare added to Holinshed's version of events surrounding Duncan's murder, inventing more than thirty details not mentioned in the "Chronicles". The first appearance of the witches, Macbeth's letter to his wife, Banquo's ghost and Lady Macbeth's sleepwalking are all products of Shakespeare's creative mind. In a masterly way, Shakespeare combined historical fact and dramatic fancy to produce an exciting spectacle enjoyed not only by the new King for whom it was first performed but also by the thousands of Londoners who made up the audiences of the Elizabethan public playhouses.

→ **to supplement** ['- - -] to add to, to make more complete
→ **compilation** collection (from different sources)
→ **to be obliged to do s.th.** to have to do s.th.
→ **to portray** [pɔː'treɪ] (here) to describe in words
→ **conspirator** [kən'spɪrətə^r] person who makes secret plans with others to harm s.o.
→ **to be victorious** to win
→ **reputation** opinion which people have about a person
→ **courageous** brave
→ **bold** showing no fear; willing to risk danger
→ **fancy** (here) fantasy; product of the imagination

You may compare the following extract from Holinshed's CHRONICLES with Shakespeare's MACBETH, Act I, Scene 3:

> Shortlie after happened a strange and uncouth woonder, which afterward was the cause of much trouble in the realme of Scotland, as ye shall after heare. It fortuned as Makbeth and Banquho journied towards Fores, where the king then laie, they went sporting by the waie togither without other

→ **uncouth** [ʌn'kuːθ] of an unknown or unfamiliar character; unusual; strange; of strange appearance
→ **realme** kingdom
→ **to fortune** (of events) to happen; to chance; to occur
→ **to sport** to amuse or recreate oneself

companie, save onelie themselves, passing thorough the woods and fields, when suddenlie in the middest of a laund, there met them three women in strange and wild apparell, resembling creatures of elder world, whome when they attentivelie beheld, woondering much at the sight, the first of them spake and said; All haile Makbeth, thane of Glammis (for he had latelie entered into that dignitie and office by the death of his father Sinell.) The second of them said; Haile Makbeth thane of Cawder. But the third said; All haile Makbeth that heereafter shalt be king of Scotland.

Macbeth, Banquo and the three weird sisters

Then Banquho; What manner of women (saith he) are you, that seeme so little favourable unto me, whereas to my fellow heere, besides high offices, ye assigne also the kingdome, appointing foorth nothing for me at all? Yes (saith the first of them) we promise greater benefits unto thee, than unto him, for he shall reigne in deed, but with an unluckie end: neither shall he leave anie issue behind him to succeed in his place, where contrarilie thou in deed shalt not reigne at all, but of thee those shall be borne which shall govern the Scottish kingdome by long order of continuall descent. Herewith the foresaid women vanished immediatlie out of their sight. This was reputed at the first but some vaine fantasticall illusion by Mackbeth and Banquho, insomuch that Banquho would call Mackbeth in jest, king of Scotland; and Mackbeth againe would call him in sport likewise, the father of manie kings. But afterwards the common opinion was, that these women were either the weird sisters, that is (as ye would say) the goddesses of destinie, or else some nymphs or feiries, indued with knowledge of prophesie by their necromanticall science, bicause everie thing came to passe as they had spoken. For shortlie after, the thane of Cawder being condemned at Fores of treason against the king committed; his lands, livings, and offices were given of the kings liberalitie to Mackbeth.

→ **by the waie** in the course of one's walk or journey; incidentally
→ **thorough** through;
→ **laund** an open space among woods; a glade
→ **apparell** clothing
→ **elder** ancient; earlier; former
→ **beheld** past tense form of 'to behold': to watch
→ **shalt be** old form of 'shall', t-ending of 2nd pers. sg.; cf. German *bis-t*; 'you will most certainly be'
→ **saith** old form of 'said', th-ending of 3rd pers. sg. (originally written þ)
→ **favourable** pleasing; gracious
→ **to assign** to allot to a person; to pass over possession of s.th., especially in law
→ **to appoint** to grant authoritatively
→ **foorth** forwards; joined to a verb: 'to go on doing' what the verb denotes
→ **benefit** a favour, gift; advantage
→ **unto** to
→ **issue** offspring, a child or children; a descendant or descendants
→ **contrarilie** on the contrary
→ **descent** [dɪ'sent] the line of family origins from one person to another in a family; lineage ['lɪni-ɪdʒ]
→ **vaine** useless; empty; of no effect, force or power
→ **fantasticall** existing only in the imagination; unreal; irrationally imagined
→ **insomuch that** to such an extent that; so that
→ **in jest** for fun; intended to excite laughter
→ **in sport** for fun; intended to excite laughter
→ **weird sisters** [wɪəd] the 3 goddesses who, according to ancient mythology, decided the course of human life; cf. 'Nornen'; from Old English *wyrd:* 'fate'; 'destiny'; some scholars think that this word once was the name of a Germanic Goddess of Fate (wurd)
→ **indued** = 'endued': supplied with anything; especially with power or quality, a spiritual gift, etc.
→ **necromanticall** having to do with the pretended art of revealing future events, etc., by means of communication with the dead; magic
→ **liberalitie** generosity

2.3. The date of the first performance of Shakespeare's MACBETH – some notes on the text

Although there is no certainty about the exact order in which Shakespeare's plays were written, modern scholars widely agree that MACBETH was completed in the year 1606. In his introduction to the Arden Shakespeare edition of MACBETH Kenneth Muir refers to the first recorded performance of MACBETH at the Globe in the spring of 1611: "Although this performance, in 1611, is the first of which we have definite record, we can be certain that the play was in existence four years before, because of echoes in contemporary plays".[5] The play must have been written after King James's coronation as King of England at Westminster in 1603 for there is an allusion in MACBETH to Banquo's descendants who are described as kings that carry "two-fold balls and treble sceptres" (IV,1,121). King James I united the crowns of England and Scotland (two-fold). The three sceptres refer to the one carried by James at the Scottish coronation to represent his authority over Scotland and the two he carried at his coronation at Westminister to represent his authority over England and Ireland.

In Act II, Scene 3 (lines 7 ff.) and in Act IV, Scene 2 (lines 45 ff.) there are allusions to an "equivocator" and to the hanging of traitors, both of which are related to the Gunpowder Plot on November 5, 1605. The aim of the plot was to blow up Parliament. Guy Fawkes and his Catholic conspirators were arrested, tried and hanged. "Equivocator" is a reference to the trial of Father Garnet, a Jesuit, on March 28, 1606 in which he defended himself by saying that he had only exercised his right of "equivocation" – saying one thing, but believing another. Thus one may conclude that the play was completed after 1603, the year of the coronation of James I, and after March 28, 1606, when Father Garnet was tried.

"It is usually supposed today that MACBETH was first performed before James I and his royal guest, King Christian IV of Denmark, some time during the latter's visit to England – 17 July to 11 August 1606. It has been argued that the performance took place at Hampton Court on 7 August 1606, one of the three occasions when Shakespeare's company acted before the kings, and this is perfectly possible."[6]

MACBETH was first published in the First Folio of 1623 which provides the basis of the modern text of the play. The First Folio version of MACBETH is far from perfect, although acts and scenes are frequently indicated. Some scholars suppose that the Folio text was printed from a prompt-book or from a written copy of such a text. The many defects of the First Folio text of MACBETH may partly be due to the fact that the printer composed Shakespeare's manuscript imperfectly. It may also have happened that the transcriber of the play, who copied it for the printer and who knew it from the stage, either reproduced blunders the actors had made on the stage or misunderstood some of their utterances.

Some shortcomings of the text may be explained by the cutting of certain passages which may have been required by the censor. There have probably been made some additions to the text to answer King James's and his contemporaries' interest in witchcraft or in burning topics of their

→ **coronation** ceremony at which a king or queen is crowned
→ **ball** orb; sphere with a cross on it carried by a king or queen as symbol of his or her authority
→ **treble** threefold; three times as much or as big as
→ **gunpowder** explosive material formerly used for firing guns
→ **Guy Fawkes** [ˌgaɪˈfɔːks]
→ **Jesuit** [ˈdʒezjʊɪt] member of the Society of Jesus, a strongly religious group within the Roman Catholic church

time (e.g. the Gun Powder Plot). The play may have been shortened in order to compensate for these additions. Among these interpolations (i.e. additions) may be the songs mentioned in the stage directions in III,5,33 and IV,1,43 which are attributed to Thomas Middleton. There is some agreement among scholars that the whole of Act III, Scene 5 and the passages in IV,1,39–43 and 125–132 were not written by Shakespeare himself.

→ **Middleton** Thomas (1570?–1627), dramatist. In his play THE WITCH (before 1627 – not published until 1778) Hecate ['hekətɪ] appears. She bears, however, no resemblance to the Hecate of MACBETH

5 Kenneth Muir. Introduction, in *Macbeth, The Arden Edition of the Works of William Shakespeare.* London: Methuen, University Paperback, 1977, repr., p. XV.

6 G. K. Hunter. Introduction, in *Macbeth, The New Penguin Shakespeare.* Harmondsworth: Penguin Paperback 1967, p. 29.

3. The Elizabethan theatre

3.1. Capacity and prices of Elizabethan public theatres[7]

In 1605 there were probably about 160,000 people living in Westminster, the City of London, and the surrounding districts. According to one estimate, in the year 1605 about 21,000 people, that is 13% of London's population, went to the theatre every week. The figure for a single day was therefore about 2,500. (It must not be forgotten that about two-thirds of the population probably never went to the theatre from one year's end to the next.)

→ **pit** space below and around an Elizabethan stage
→ **d.** from Lat. *denarius* (old) penny (pence)
→ **s.** shilling (= 12 pence) [**L** pound (= 20 shillings or 240 pence)]
→ **artisan** [ˌɑːtɪˈzæn] skilled workman
→ **quart** [ɔː] (= 2 pints)
→ 1,137 litre

There are differing estimates of the audience capacity of the various theatres. In 1596 the Dutch visitor Johannes de Witt noted that the largest of the five public theatres then existing, the Swan, could hold 3,000 people. This figure may be too high, but some of the other theatres are now believed to have had almost as great a capacity. The Fortune and the Rose had a total audience capacity of 2,344 and 2,500 respectively. Alfred Harbage maintains that in 1595 the Rose enjoyed an average daily attendance of 1,157 to 1,250 people. The private theatres probably had a capacity of about 1,000 persons each.

The price of admission at the public theatres was low enough for ordinary craftsmen and workmen to afford. It was a penny per person for standing room in the pit or yard, which was a good place for watching the play if the weather was fine. Another penny was charged if the visitor passed from the yard to the seats in the galleries. A third penny had to be paid at another door if the visitor wanted a comfortable seat in the painted galleries just above the stage, the so-called "lords' rooms" or "boxes".

In Shakespeare's time 3d. was the price of the cheapest fixed-price dinner, or of a small pipeload of tobacco. The lowest price at the "private" theatres was 6d. per person – rather high for an ordinary artisan or craftsman. In 1614 between 2d. and 3d. were paid for a quart of beer. According to Alfred Harbage the average weekly wage of a London workman in 1601 was 7s.

7 The facts and figures given in this text are mostly taken from Harbage, pp. 24–44, 55–59.

3.2. The Elizabethan public playhouse

The first public playhouse, that is the first building designed for the sole purpose of presenting plays to an audience, was built by James Burbage in 1576. It is impossible to say what it looked like exactly as no detailed drawings or written descriptions exist. Yet we can make a fairly good guess from what we know of the development of the English stage in the Elizabethan and Jacobean periods. It is more than likely that Burbage took the bear-baiting arenas of 16th century London as his model when he designed the Theatre. He probably had the pit paved so that, if it rained, the water would drain off and not collect in puddles. The stage

→ **to pave** to cover (a piece of ground or path) with stones
→ **puddle** [ʌ] small area of water on the ground where rain has collected

Arend van Bushell's copy

The Swan Theatre

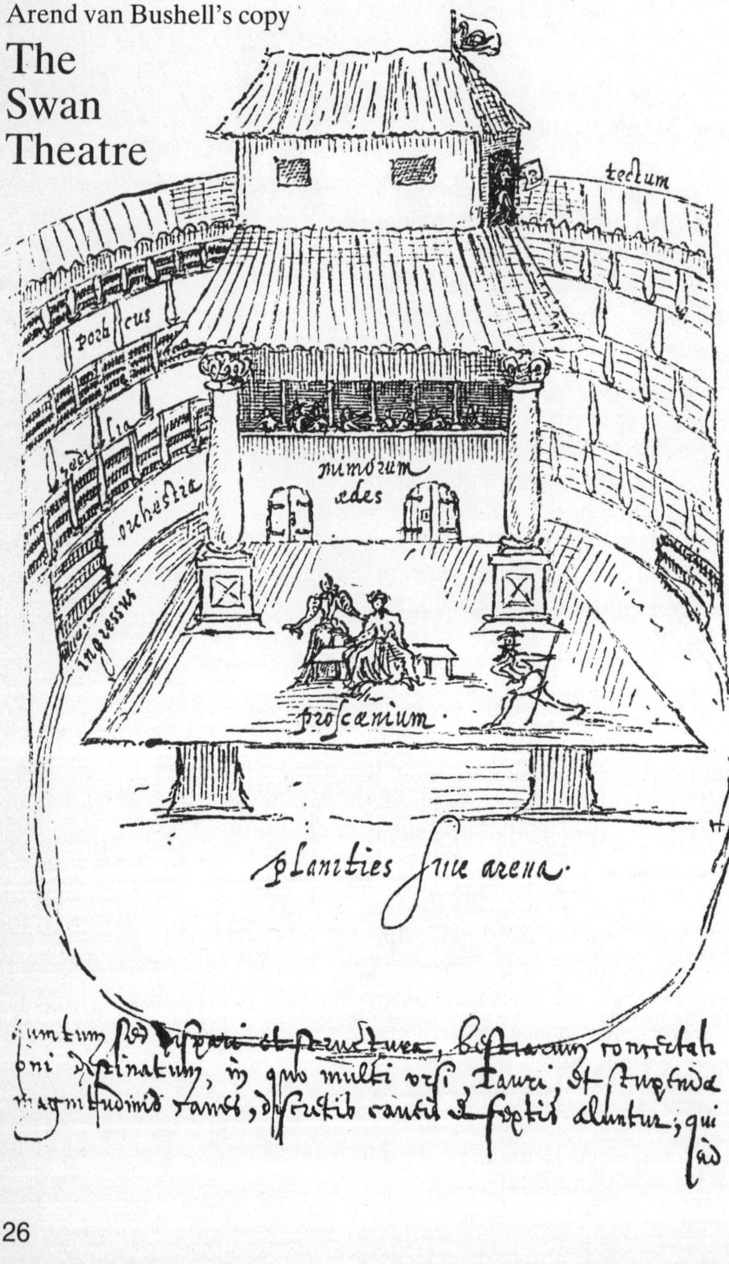

The Latin names of the different parts of the theatre have the following meanings:

tectum roof
mimorum aedes room for the players
proscoenium front stage
planities sive arena flat plain or sandy part
ingressus entrance
porticus gallery with columns
sedilia seats, benches
orchestra "the senators' or noblemen's places in a theatre"[9]

would have been quite large, providing a wide and permanent acting space for his players. In order to protect at least the back of the stage from rain, Burbage almost certainly built a roof, supported at the front by pillars, which served both as the heavens and, if needed, a place from which characters could descend onto the stage. There was also probably

→ **pillar** high, usually round, stone structure built to support a roof

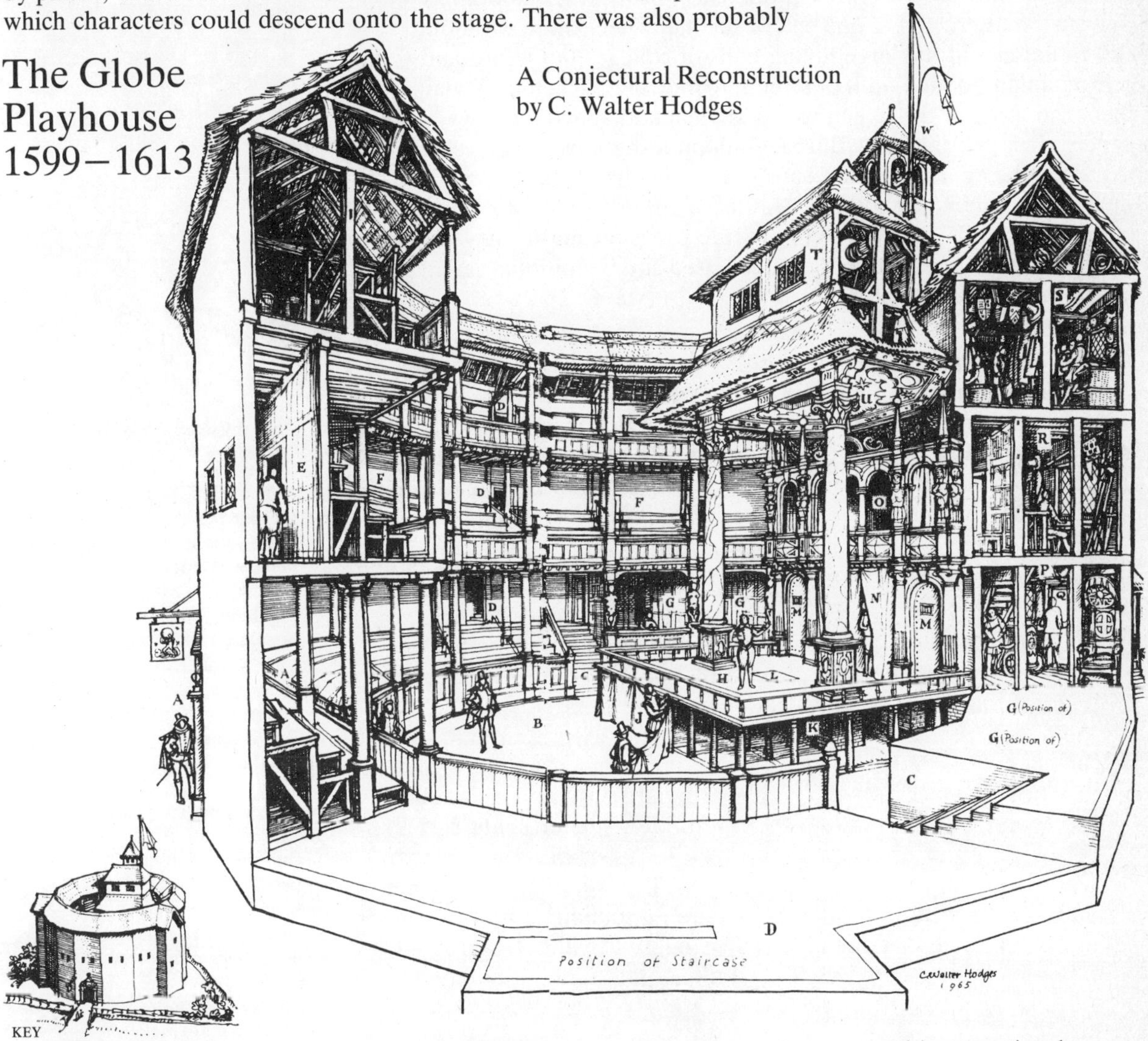

The Globe Playhouse 1599–1613

A Conjectural Reconstruction by C. Walter Hodges

KEY

- AA Main entrance
- B The Yard, where the "groundings" stood (for one penny admission)
- CC Entrances to lowest gallery (on payment of another penny)
- D Entrances to staircase and upper galleries
- E Corridor serving the different sections of the middle gallery
- F Middle gallery (The "Twopenny Rooms")
- G "Gentlemen's Rooms" or "Lords' Rooms"
- H The stage
- J The hanging being put up round the stage (N.B. In some theatres this was boarded in)
- K The "Hell" under the stage
- L The stage trap, leading down to the Hell
- MM Stage doors, leading into the tiring-house
- N Curtained "place behind the stage", sometimes opened for special scenes.
- O Gallery above the stage, used as required sometimes by musicians, sometimes by spectators, and often as part of the play (e.g. *Romeo and Juliet*)
- P Back-stages area (the tiring-house)
- Q Tiring-house door
- R Dressing rooms
- S Wardrobe and storage
- T The hut housing the machine for lowering enthroned gods, etc., to the stage
- U The "Heavens"
- W Hoisting the playhouse flag

at least one trapdoor in the floor of the stage so that characters could appear from below.

Burbage may have also borrowed ideas from the private performances of plays before invited audiences in the halls of colleges, schools and so on. The stage was erected at one end of the hall where there was often, as is still to be seen in the large dining-halls of colleges in Oxford and Cambridge, a thin wooden wall, or screen, to hide the kitchen from view. Two doors led through the screen to the kitchen and above there was a small gallery. It is possible that Burbage adopted the idea of the screen, the two doors being used for the entrances and exits of the actors while the small gallery above could have been used either to seat prominent spectators (the "lords' room") or to provide room for musicians (the "minstrels' room"). It could also have been used as an additional acting plain, for example in balcony scenes.

All this, however, is speculation. Not one of the public playhouses has survived and archaeological evidence is meagre. One of the most important documents on the Elizabethan stage that have been preserved is a sketch of the interior of the Swan theatre as it was in 1596, twenty years after the building of Burbage's Theatre. In that year a Dutchman, Johann de Witt, visited London and seems to have been particularly interested in the public playhouses there. In his diary he wrote:

> There are four amphitheatres in London of notable beauty, which from their diverse signs bear diverse names. In each of them a different play is daily exhibited to the populace. The two more magnificent of these are situated to the southward beyond the Thames, and from the signs suspended before them are called the Rose and the Swan. . . . Of all the theatres, however, the largest and the most magnificent is that one of which the sign is a swan, called in the vernacular the Swan Theatre; for it accommodates in its seats three thousand persons, and is built of a mass of flint stones (of which there is a prodigious supply in Britain), and supported by wooden columns painted in such excellent imitation of marble that it is able to deceive even the most cunning. Since its form resembles that of a Roman work, I have made a sketch of it.[8]

Unfortunately, his original sketch has been lost and all that has survived is a copy of it by Arend van Bushell, the accuracy of which, moreover, is questioned by experts.

Various Shakespeare scholars have attempted to make a drawing of an Elizabethan theatre. Perhaps the most detailed is C. W. Hodges's reconstruction of the Globe theatre, the theatre which James Burbage built when the lease of the Theatre expired in 1598 and (the theatre) which was to become famous for the staging of Shakespeare's plays.

8 quoted from: Gurr, p. 89
9 Harbage, p. 25

→ **trapdoor** doorway in the floor through which one can climb from one level to another by a stairs or ladder

Middle Temple Hall, London

→ **meagre** [iː] not much, not enough
→ **to preserve** to keep s.th. for a long time (by looking after it)
→ **sketch** picture drawn (perhaps quickly) without too much detail
→ **notable** remarkable
→ **diverse** [daɪˈvɜːs] different
→ **to exhibit** to show
→ **populace** the ordinary people; the general public
→ **to suspend** [–ˈ–] to hang
→ **vernacular** [vəˈnækjʊləʳ] native language of a country as opposed to a foreign language (e.g. Latin) that was often used in writing
→ **to accommodate** have or provide seats for
→ **flint stone** Kieselstein
→ **prodigious** [prəˈdɪdʒəs] enormous, great
→ **column** [ɒ] pillar (see above) sometimes standing alone as a monument
→ **marble** Marmor
→ **to deceive** to make s.o. believe s.th. which is false
→ **cunning** (here, old use) persons having great knowledge; knowing very much
→ **accuracy** [ˈækjərəsi] exactness; correctness in every detail
→ **lease** contract by which a person pays money (usually a rent) to use land, buildings, etc. which he does not own
→ **to expire** to come to an end
→ **to stage** to perform (a play) on a stage

3.3. The origins of the Elizabethan stage

Medieval drama arose in the first place from the church's search for new and more effective ways of spreading the word of God. For centuries, the only means the clergy possessed to illustrate the events of the Bible were the stained-glass windows of the church itself. As early as the 10th century, however, short dramatic representations of biblical scenes such as the birth and death of Christ (MYSTERY PLAYS) were performed at the corresponding time of year. Also the lives of saints were portrayed and in the course of time (from the 12th to the 15th century) short plays were performed, at first in Latin, later in English, which are known as MIRACLE PLAYS.

With the staging of more complex plays, more scenes were necessary and scenery was put up in different locations of the church; these were called "mansions" or "houses". They served the purpose of representing heaven, hell or hell-gate and the palaces of Herod or Pilate, etc. These mansions were at first placed within the church but in time, as the organization and acting of the plays passed from the clergy to the guilds, which were associations of craftsmen, the wooden structures or boxes of the mansions were placed outside the church building, eventually in a row or in a half circle. Each mansion represented a scene in the story to be told and each had its own group of actors. The action passed from one mansion to another, the actors leaving the mansion at the start of the scene and returning to it at the end. Most of the action, therefore, took place in the area in front of and between the mansions, the so-called "playne", which had, unlike the mansions, no definite location such as heaven or hell. It was the actors' task, when they were in the "playne", to convey the location of a particular scene to the audience by words and gestures.

A variation of this method of presentation was the "pageant" (from Latin "pagina" = 'a plank of wood'). Mansions were mounted on four-wheeled waggons and rolled through the streets while the audience stayed where they were. One after another the waggons arrived and the actors played their scene before moving on to the next stage of their journey through the town. Each pageant carried a two-storied wooden structure consisting of four vertical poles, one at each corner, linked by horizontal bars and strong boards which formed the roof of the lower and the floor of the upper storey. The upper storey had no roof. Curtains were fitted in such a way that the whole structure, or parts of it, could be hidden from or presented to the audience's view as the actors desired. The two storeys could be used to perform actions which were intended to take place on a city wall or at a window (upper storey) or on the ground floor of a house in one of its rooms (lower storey). Although the curtains of the lower storey were usually kept open, they were closed when the players entered or left the stage. Some scholars believe that the lower storey was used as a tiring-room where the actors changed their costumes; others claim that the tiring-room was underneath the pageant, between the lower storey and the ground.

In the course of the 15th and 16th centuries the Miracle Plays were largely replaced by Morality Plays. These intended to teach a moral by

→ **clergy** all the religious officials who are authorized to hold a church service
→ **stained-glass windows** windows often showing a picture (esp. in churches) made of differently coloured glass
→ **location** place
→ **craftsman** worker who produces things from stone, metal, etc.
→ **playne** plain, a large stretch of flat ground (land)
→ **to convey** carry (from one place to another); (here) communicate
→ **two-storied** having two floors (storeys) or levels
→ **tiring-room** (from **to tire** to dress up, to decorate) dressing-room

showing the struggle of virtue against vice. Abstract notions, such as Death, Goodness, Knowledge or Sin, appeared on the stage as persons. At the same time the Interludes had become popular. These had been performed since the 14th century and consisted mainly of short and witty dialogues which were meant not only as comic relief between other forms of entertainment but also as social, religious or even political satire. Both of these kinds of play were performed either by townsmen or by students and professional entertainers who travelled from place to place.

The stages on which these plays were performed were temporary and, if they were not put up in public places, they were more often than not to be found in the yards of large inns. These yards were U-shaped, meaning that they had two long walls opposite each other with a short wall linking them. Two pageants were placed against one of the long walls at some distance to each other and a small platform on planks, supported by strong beams and perhaps barrels, was erected between them.

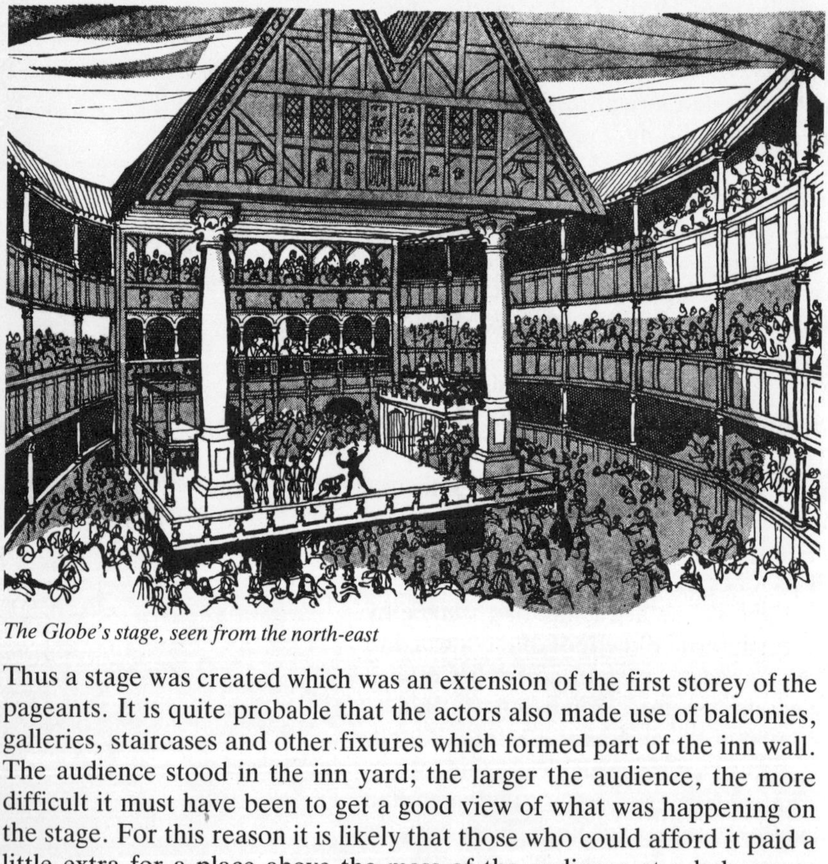

The Globe's stage, seen from the north-east

Thus a stage was created which was an extension of the first storey of the pageants. It is quite probable that the actors also made use of balconies, galleries, staircases and other fixtures which formed part of the inn wall. The audience stood in the inn yard; the larger the audience, the more difficult it must have been to get a good view of what was happening on the stage. For this reason it is likely that those who could afford it paid a little extra for a place above the mass of the audience at a balcony or gallery on the wall facing the stage or on the one at right angles to it.

The platform between the two pageants became more and more important as the stage on which the action took place; it became wider and deeper, jutting into the so-called "pit", the area occupied by the audience, and, like the "playne" mentioned above, it was a sort of neutral ground, having no specific locality and depending on the words and

→ **virtue** any good quality of character or behaviour (Tugend)
→ **vice** wickedness of character (Laster)
→ **notion** idea, concept
→ **temporary** ['tempərəri] existing or lasting for a limited time only
→ **to link** to join
→ **plank** long, thin piece of wood used to make a floor
→ **beam** [i:] strong, thick piece of wood used to support s.th.
→ **barrel** large, round, wooden or metal container used for transporting beer, oil, etc.
→ **extension** part which is added on to s.th. to make it bigger or longer
→ **at right angles** ['æŋgəlz] at an angle (Winkel) of 90°
→ **to jut** [dʒʌt] to stand out or forward

gestures of the actors to give it its time and place. Correspondingly, the two pageants became less and less important. L. Hotson[10] maintains that, as "transparent 'rooms' standing over the trapdoors of entrance", they were placed on the opposite sides of the oblong Elizabethan stage. There they faced each other either singly or in two rows of several wooden structures whose two storeys could be kept open or closed to the audience's view, representing city walls or upper and lower storeys of houses during the dramatic action on the main stage between them. R. Hosley[11] argues that by Shakespeare's time pageants had long ceased to be used as stages for dramatic purposes and that raised one-storied structures, so-called "booth stages" were used instead. Whereas the pageants were stable wooden structures the booths were makeshift "huts" without roofs and with walls of canvas hung between four posts. These booths, like the pageants, could be erected in the market place or in inn yards and bull- and bear-baiting arenas singly or placed side by side to form a bigger stage. They, too, could be curtained off from the audience and were the means by which actors entered and left the stage.

As was mentioned earlier, the stages were also put up in public places. One great disadvantage of this was the difficulty of getting money from the audience and the players soon realized that it was better to perform their plays in an enclosed space with an entrance at which the spectators had to pay before they could enter. Inn yards were an obvious choice since inns were places which always attracted crowds, but there were other locations which were even more practical than these. The baiting of bulls and bears (which were still common in Europe at the time) was a popular sport in the Elizabethan age. The animals were chained to a wooden post in the ground and then attacked and bitten to death after a furious fight, by dogs. These spectacles took place in bear gardens, oval-shaped arenas consisting of a pit, where the fight took place, and two or three tiers of galleries for the spectators. At least one similar bear-baiting arena was to be found to the south of the City of London, on the Bankside. It appears that bear gardens were also used by companies of actors for the performance of plays. A booth stage was erected in one of the sharply rounded curves of the oval and the audience either stood around the stage or, if they could afford it, sat in the more expensive galleries.

The stages erected in inn yards or in bear gardens were the beginnings of the Elizabethan public theatre. They were not permanent homes for companies of actors, nor were they weather-proof. They served, however, as models for the public playhouses which were to spring up in London at the end of the 16th and the beginning of the 17th centuries.

→ **oblong** ['ɒblɒŋ] (a figure) with 4 straight sides, forming 4 right angles, which is longer than it is wide
→ **stable** firm
→ **makeshift** provisional; used at the time because nothing better can be found
→ **canvas** ['––] strong rough cloth used for tents, sails, bags, etc.
→ **to bait** [eɪ] to provoke and attack by hitting
→ **tier** [tɪə^{r}] one of a number of rows arranged one on top of the other
→ **permanent** ['pɜ:mənənt] existing or lasting for an unlimited time (opposite of temporary)
→ **weather-proof** ready for use in all kinds of weather; independent of the weather

10 Leslie Hotson, *Shakespeare's Wooden O.* London: Rupert Hart-Davies, 1960, p. 153.
11 Richard Hosley, "Theaterbauten und Bühne", in *Shakespeare: Eine Einführung,* eds. Kenneth Muir, Samuel Schoenbaum et. al. Stuttgart: Philipp Reclam jun., 1972, p. 20ff.

4. From manuscript to performance of a play[12]

4.1. Revision and collaboration

Shakespeare may have started his career by adapting popular older plays, and making whatever additions seemed desirable. Many Elizabethan dramatists used to re-write plays for actors' companies as well as selling them original ones of their own. Such playwrights often collaborated in so-called "syndicates" for the writing of new plays and the revision of old ones.

→ **syndicate** ['sɪndɪkeɪt] a group of people combined together for a particular purpose, especially, making money
→ **TITUS ANDRONICUS** ['taɪtəs æn'drɒnɪkəs]
→ **to pacify** to make calm

There are some examples of revision and collaboration in Shakespeare's own works. His play Love's Labour's Lost, for example, is described on its title-page as "Newly corrected and augmented by W. Shakespeare", while Titus Andronicus and The Merry Wives of Windsor show signs of having been revised either by Shakespeare himself or by somebody else. Sir Thomas More, a play which is thought to be in part by Shakespeare, was written or revised by no fewer than six different persons. The particular scene attributed to Shakespeare consists of three manuscript pages. It is a scene in which More pacifies a gang of rioters. The handwriting and spelling of this passage have been identified as Shakespeare's; moreover, in style and atmosphere it resembles certain crowd scenes in his own plays. As for Macbeth, most scholars agree that the bleeding sergeant's speech in I,2, and the Hecate scenes (III,5 and part of IV,1) were not written by Shakespeare himself.

4.2. Foul papers and fair copies

Shakespeare's original editors Heminge and Condell, writing seven years after his death, declared that they had "scarce received from him a blot in his papers"[13]. This strongly suggests that some at least of Shakespeare's own manuscripts were still in existence in or shortly before 1623. Today, however, apart from the three pages of the Sir Thomas More manuscript mentioned above (an attribution that is of course not absolutely certain), all Shakespeare's literary and dramatic manuscripts have disappeared.

→ **deletion** [dɪ'liːʃən] s.th. crossed out

What form did his original manuscripts take? Obviously when he was writing a play he must have made corrections and improvements to his rough copy. Scholars believe that in some cases these "foul papers", with many deletions and with corrections inserted between the lines, served as copy text for early Quartos: for such editions appear to contain errors that derive from the original manuscript.

It is believed that in other cases a "fair copy" was made from Shakespeare's rough copy by a professional copyist, who corrected any errors he came across as he copied. This "fair copy" would later be offered for sale to a players' company. Elizabethan dramatists generally wrote their plays for actors' companies, who bought the plays and paid for them at once. Thus many authors preferred having their plays acted on the stage to having them printed.

4.3. Author's copyright

When an Elizabethan dramatist sold a manuscript to an actors' company for production on the stage he often practically lost both his copyright and any control over the staging and printing of his play. The manuscript and the play itself became the property of the actors' company, so that the actors could give the author permission to have the work printed, or else sell their rights in the play to a printer quite independently of the author. They might even decide to publish it themselves. This is what happened when after Shakespeare's death the First Folio of his plays was published. It was Shakespeare's fellow-actors, the partners in the company to which he himself had belonged, who decided upon and organized its publication.

As a rule the members of an Elizabethan actors' company kept their copyright to a play as long as it continued to attract good audiences. They could generally make a larger profit by performing the work to full houses than by selling the fair copy to a printer or publishing the text themselves.

4.4. A book-keeper's different functions and the prompt-book

Whenever an actors' company bought a play, the manuscript would be handed over to the "book-keeper", whose duty it was to keep the fair copy safe. The book-keeper was often also the prompter, the man who held the "book" or "prompt-book" during performances and whose job it was to remind the actors of their words whenever they forgot them. In some cases the book-keeper (or "book-holder") may also have prepared the fair copy for his work as a prompter. He then made a "prompt-book" (or "prompt-copy") of the manuscript by adding directions and cues for the actors. The book-keeper may also have had the tasks of a stage manager who wrote in stage directions or notes for the effective use of smoke, thunder and other noises, or of weapons, lanterns and other stage props, and any stage furniture. In other cases the book-keeper may also have had the important function of checking the fair copy in order to make sure that it contained no attacks on religion or the government, and no indecencies. If he came across such potentially offensive passages he had to cross them out before taking the manuscript to the official censor (see: 4.7. "The Master of the Revels and the Revels Office").

→ **prop** [ɒ] any small article used on the stage during the acting of the play
→ **indecency** [ɪn'diːsənsi] words, etc., that are likely to be found shocking for reasons of sexual morality or good taste
→ **revels** ['revəlz]: merry-making with dancing, games, masquing, acting, etc.

4.5. Copyist, author and the prompt-book

It is believed that usually not the book-keeper but some copyist or even the author himself made changes in the fair copy to prepare it for the stage. Then the copyist would make a new copy with all the stage directions, and notes for the use of props, etc. In this manner many a prompt-book came into being. The prompt-book was then sent with a fixed fee to the official censor, the Master of the Revels who had to read and consider the play, crossing out any passages that struck him as unacceptable. At last he sent it back to the actors' company with a performing licence. This text (or a copy of it) was afterwards used as the authoritative text of the play and was of course used by the prompter at all performances.

→ **authoritative** [–'– – – –] accepted by everyone as correct and reliable

4.6. Plot and actors' parts

To help the actors and stage hands the copyist may then have prepared a "plot" of the play from the prompt-book. The "plot" was a general outline of all the scenes in the play, listing the different characters appearing in each and the main points of the stage directions (exits, entrances, noises, stage props, etc.). For convenience the two sheets of paper on which all this was written were glued to the two sides of a thin board which was hung where it could be taken down whenever it was needed.

→ **stage hands** the stage manager's assistants

To assist the actors in remembering their lines the copyist also transcribed each actor's entire "part" for him. The sheets containing the actor's lines (with some of his cues and some stage directions) were glued together in such a way that they formed a roll about five cm wide and five m long. Some of the actors wrote in their own improvements and corrections to the text on these rolls. These alterations had an influence on the printed versions of the plays.

4.7. The Master of the Revels and the Revels Office

In Elizabethan times no play could be performed unless it had been passed by the censor. In 1559 Queen Elizabeth had given the task of examining and censoring plays to the local mayors (in the case of towns) and the local justices of the peace (in the country). It thus became their duty to examine plays and to suppress any passages that either seemed likely to offend people's moral or religious feelings or contained direct or indirect criticism of the government. In London at least, the civic authorities proved unsatisfactory censors. They abused their powers and tried to suppress plays altogether, even outside the city boundaries. So in 1581 the Queen decided to appoint her Master of the Revels dramatic censor for the whole of England. The Master of the Revels was the official of the royal household who was responsible for organizing the court entertainments, which included sports, masques, and other theatrical performances. The post had originally been only a part-time one, but with the growing importance of the London theatres the Master's duties came to occupy his entire time and he himself gained in power and importance. He was in charge of the "Revels Office", whose purpose it was to direct those who provided the costumes, sets, and anything else that might be needed, and to make sure that the actors and workmen were paid and the payments recorded in the "Revels Accounts".

→ **masque** [ma:sk] a type of play often performed in the 16th and 17th centuries for kings, queens, or noblemen, written in verse, with music, dancing and songs
→ **sets** painted backgrounds

4.8. Lord Chamberlain and Privy Council

The Master of the Revels with his Revels Office belonged to the department of the "Lord Chamberlain", who was responsible for the smooth running of the royal household. Thus the rooms in the royal palaces, the royal clothes, and the welcoming and accommodation of royal visitors and high-ranking representatives of foreign countries were all the Lord Chamberlain's responsibility. His authority also extended to the entertainment of the Queen and her guests with music, dancing, masques, and performing of plays.

→ **privy** ['prɪvi] (old use) secret, private

The Lord Chamberlain was one of the eleven personal advisers to the Queen who together formed the "Privy Council", the highest law-administering and decision-making body in the land. From 1594 to 1603 Shakespeare and the other actors of the "Chamberlain's Men" enjoyed the protection of this extremely powerful patron. The Privy Council as well as the Lord Chamberlain was concerned in the censorship of plays and the control of dramatic performances. The Master of the Revels' powers of censorship were extended in 1607 when he was given control over the printing of all plays.

It is interesting to note that the Queen took the side of the actors' companies against the protests of the Puritans who were doing all they could to prevent or to limit the acting of plays. As the Privy Council followed her wishes its decisions often served to protect the actors and their companies.

Tiring-House, 'House', and 'Above'

12 For the information given in chapters 4. and 5. the author is particularly indebted to: G. B. Harrison, *Introducing Shakespeare,* Harmondsworth: Penguin Books Ltd., 1977, 3rd edition, repr. and to: Campbell/Quinn.

13 J. Heminge and H. Condell, "To The Great Variety of Readers", in *William Shakespeare: The Complete Works,* ed. Peter Alexander. London and Glasgow: Collins, 1951, p. XXVII.

5. From performance to printing of a play

5.1. Publisher's copyright and the Stationers' Company

By buying a play an actors' company acquired the right to publish it or to authorize the author to do so. But in practice the actors often sold their rights to a printer without consulting the author. Apart from a few cases in which a playwright was given the right to control the publication of his works, there was virtually no author's copyright in Shakespeare's day.

→ **stationer** ['steɪʃənə^{r}] (old use) bookseller who also publishes
→ **virtually** very nearly, in effect, practically

Generally when a printer bought a manuscript from one of the actors' companies he tried to get his copyright established with the "Stationers' Company". Since its foundation in 1557 this organization of publishers and printers had exercised undivided control over the English printing trade, not only deciding quarrels between its members but also granting publisher's copyright. Before the Company gave one of its members permission to publish a manuscript that he had bought, this had to be examined and licensed by the Archbishop of Canterbury – in practice by a member of his staff appointed for this purpose. Only after the permission to print the manuscript had been obtained from the Archbishop of Canterbury, or the Bishop of London, or a member of the Privy Council could the court of the Stationers' Company grant copyright to a printer. By the rules of the Stationers' Company a printer had to ask the Company's clerk to enter the title of the work he intended to publish in the "Stationers' Register".

5.2. Pirated editions – the bad Quartos

A printer who "pirated" a popular Shakespeare play was likely to produce a text that was full of mistakes, a so-called "bad" Quarto. He may have bought the manuscript from someone who had stolen it from the actors' company. Or perhaps some actors who needed money had sold copies of their parts to the publisher. Or else, former members of Shakespeare's company or actors of small roles in one of his plays may have reproduced a confused and corrupt text of the whole play from memory, but with their own less important parts more accurately reproduced. Scholars call such texts "memorial reconstructions". But not all critics accept these theories, which remain unsupported by satisfactory evidence. Another theory is that people employed by the publisher attended plays as members of the audience and took down the text in shorthand. i.e. writing rapidly and using a system of signs or shorter forms for letters, words and phrases. But the existence of such "stenographic reports" has been called in question, for it would surely have been extremely difficult for anybody to take down a play without getting detected. Another difficulty about this theory is that there was no really adequate system of shorthand in Shakespeare's time though books on the subject appeared towards the end of the 16th century.

→ **to pirate** ['paɪərət] to make and sell (a book, etc.) without permission or payment
→ **shorthand** a system of writing quickly, making use of signs or shorter forms for letters, words, etc.
→ **hack** a literary man who lives by doing work of the lowest sort

However the publishers of the "bad" Quartos obtained their texts – one thing is certain: they published them without informing the actors who were the rightful owners of the works, or asking the consent of the author. Sometimes, no doubt, a hack was employed to put a text together from a number of incomplete manuscripts which were all more or less different from the original and full of every kind of error. These corrupt texts were often reprinted with scarcely any alterations.

→ **surreptitious** [ˌsərəp'tɪʃəs] made secretly and dishonestly
→ **to maim** [maɪm] to harm a part of the body so that it cannot be used; maimed (here) incomplete and corrupt
→ **stealth** ['stelθ] secrecy

Athough the "bad" Quartos are not all equally bad they show similar characteristics which mark them out as highly corrupt: passages that are repeated in a confused way, giving a false idea of the meaning of the text ("garbled passages"), omissions, and passages not by Shakespeare ("interpolations").

It is not known for certain how many of Shakespeare's plays had been issued in pirated editions before the "First Folio Edition" of his works in 1623, but the figure is at least seven. A few scholars put it as high as eight or ten. The preface to the First Folio (by Shakespeare's fellow-actors John Heminge and Henry Condell) mentions these "stolen and surreptitious copies, maimed, and deformed by . . . frauds and stealths".[14] The Folio editors claimed that their edition offered the pirated plays "cured and perfect", and that all the others were exactly "as he (Shakespeare) conceived them".

14 Heminge/Condell, in Alexander, p. XXVII.

5.3. Quarto and folio formats

The term "quarto" describes the way in which the pages of the book were printed and folded before being bound. In a quarto volume each large sheet of paper is folded twice in order to produce four leaves. As two pages are always printed on each leaf (one on the front and the other on the back) one quarto sheet contains eight pages of print. In Shakespeare's day plays and other short books were normally printed in quarto, whereas longer books were usually printed in folio. The folio format involves folding a single sheet of paper in such a way that it forms two leaves or four pages.

5.4. The good Quartos

→ **to usurp** [ju:'zɜ:p]: to seize for oneself, especially unlawfully

Sometimes when the rights of Shakespeare and his fellow-actors were usurped by the appearance of pirated editions they reacted by publishing the authorized texts themselves. The plays involved were those that had been performed many times and had become especially popular. Fourteen of these authorized editions were published during Shakespeare's lifetime. They are known as the "good" Quartos and though they vary in quality they present a definite contrast to the pirated versions. There are, however, only two Shakespeare plays for which we have both a "good" and a "bad" Quarto, ROMEO AND JULIET and HAMLET. Even the good Quartos were somehow treated as merely provisional, for Shakespeare did not bother to supervise their publication himself. He did not correct the "proofs" (the sheets printed at the very beginning so that any mistakes could be put right before the proper printing of the edition began). Without the author's supervision and proof-reading a printer was sometimes unable to cope properly with all the difficulties presented by the different kinds of copy (foul papers, fair copies, prompt-books, etc.). He may even have had before him a manuscript copy prepared by a professional copyist for the library of some gentleman who was interested in literature in general and in Shakespeare's work in particular. It is therefore hardly surprising that even the good Quartos are not free from faults and varying degrees of corruption, for during the printing process they, too, became altered and distorted. A printer's willingness to struggle with difficult handwriting, his ability to make intelligent guesses, and the care he took when reading proofs depended on his interest in, and knowledge of the text. The quality of a particular edition is also dependent on the printer's powers of concentration, level of education, general knowledge, and skill.

5.5. Some editions of Shakespeare's plays:

5.5.1. The Folio Editions

When in 1623 Shakespeare's old friends and fellow-actors John Heminge and Henry Condell attempted the first complete edition of Shakespeare's plays they published 36 of them. For 18 of these plays the First Folio is the only authoritative text, as they had never been printed before. The volume is known as the First Folio to distinguish it from the later folio editions of 1632, 1663/4, and 1685.

In the First Folio the comedies, histories, and tragedies form three different sections with separately numbered pages. Only the histories are arranged chronologically. The editors based their work on manuscripts of various kinds and in some cases on earlier editions, including the "good" Quartos. Heminge and Condell may also have used manuscripts copied from "foul" or "fair" papers or some other text that had never been used for theatrical purposes. The First Folio editors also turned to the "bad" Quartos with their pirated and corrupt texts. Although Heminge and Condell tried to avoid errors by comparing the published Quartos with manuscripts they owned they did so unmethodically and carelessly. According to one scholarly account, in cases where there was no complete manuscript, "prompt-book", or printed text of a play they put together an "assembled text" of their own from the various actors' "parts" and the prompter's shortened version of the play (the "plot") integrating the different elements into a single text.

As some of the material the editors used had never been intended for the printer, the First Folio inevitably included certain defects taken over from these.

While arranging the pages for printing the printer may sometimes have misinterpreted foul papers or one of the prompt-books because of the author's or copyist's bad handwriting, or because of the many corrections and additions to the text. Occasionally a slip of paper may have got lost, or else the printer may not have had room to insert the additions without cutting out something else. Thus there was a jump of thought in the newly printed text. In other cases the same passage was printed twice, first uncorrected and then corrected by the printer. Although printing in

→ **compositor** [kəm'pɒzɨtəʳ] a printer who actually forms words, sentences, etc. out of metal type, ready for printing

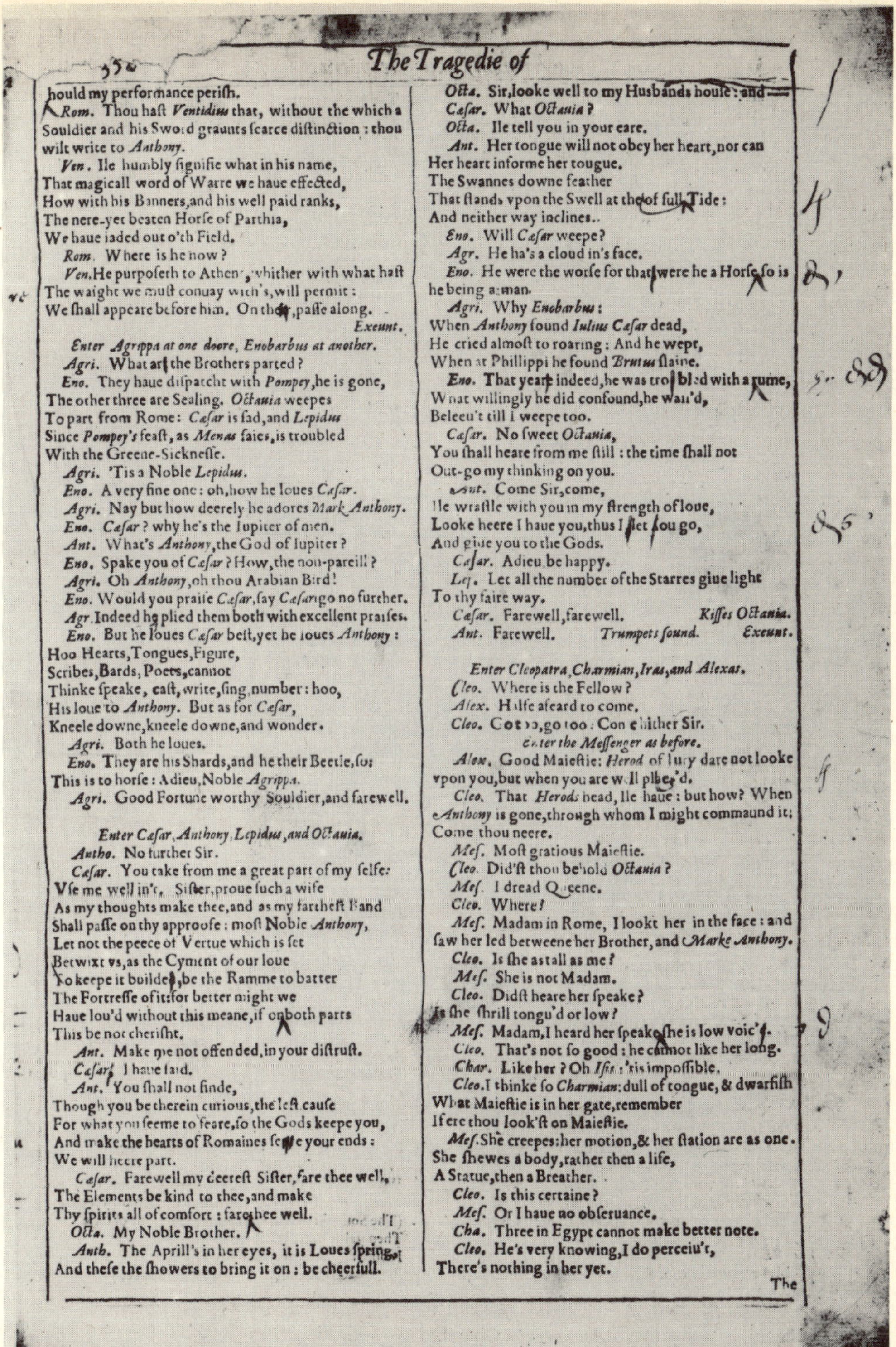

350 The Tragedie of

hould my performance periſh.
Rom. Thou haſt *Ventidius* that, without the which a Souldier and his Sword graunts ſcarce diſtinction: thou wilt write to *Anthony.*
Ven. Ile humbly ſignifie what in his name,
That magicall word of Warre we haue effected,
How with his Banners,and his well paid ranks,
The nere-yet beaten Horſe of Parthia,
We haue iaded out o'th Field.
Rom. Where is he now?
Ven. He purpoſeth to Athens, whither with what haſt
The waight we muſt conuay with's,will permit:
We ſhall appeare before him. On there,paſſe along.
Exeunt.

Enter Agrippa at one doore, Enobarbus at another.

Agri. What are the Brothers parted?
Eno. They haue diſpatcht with *Pompey*,he is gone,
The other three are Sealing. *Octauia* weepes
To part from Rome: *Cæſar* is ſad,and *Lepidus*
Since *Pompey's* feaſt, as *Menas* ſaies,is troubled
With the Greene-Sickneſſe.
Agri. 'Tis a Noble *Lepidus.*
Eno. A very fine one: oh,how he loues *Cæſar.*
Agri. Nay but how deerely he adores *Mark Anthony.*
Eno. *Cæſar*? why he's the Iupiter of men.
Ant. What's *Anthony*,the God of Iupiter?
Eno. Spake you of *Cæſar*? How,the non-pareill?
Agri. Oh *Anthony*,oh thou Arabian Bird!
Eno. Would you praiſe *Cæſar*,ſay *Cæſar* go no further.
Agr. Indeed he plied them both with excellent praiſes.
Eno. But he loues *Cæſar* beſt,yet he loues *Anthony*:
Hoo Hearts,Tongues,Figure,
Scribes,Bards,Poets,cannot
Thinke ſpeake, caſt,write,ſing,number: hoo,
His loue to *Anthony.* But as for *Cæſar*,
Kneele downe,kneele downe,and wonder.
Agri. Both he loues.
Eno. They are his Shards,and he their Beetle,ſo:
This is to horſe: Adieu,Noble *Agrippa.*
Agri. Good Fortune worthy Souldier,and farewell.

Enter Cæſar,Anthony,Lepidus,and Octauia.

Antho. No further Sir.
Cæſar. You take from me a great part of my ſelfe:
Vſe me well in't. Siſter,proue ſuch a wife
As my thoughts make thee,and as my fartheſt Band
Shall paſſe on thy approofe: moſt Noble *Anthony*,
Let not the peece of Vertue which is ſet
Betwixt vs,as the Cyment of our loue
To keepe it builded,be the Ramme to batter
The Fortreſſe of it:for better might we
Haue lou'd without this meane,if on both parts
This be not cheriſht.
Ant. Make me not offended,in your diſtruſt.
Cæſar. I haue ſaid.
Ant. You ſhall not finde,
Though you be therein curious,the leſt cauſe
For what you ſeeme to feare,ſo the Gods keepe you,
And make the hearts of Romaines ſerue your ends:
We will heere part.
Cæſar. Farewell my deereſt Siſter,fare thee well,
The Elements be kind to thee,and make
Thy ſpirits all of comfort: fare thee well.
Octa. My Noble Brother.
Anth. The Aprill's in her eyes, it is Loues ſpring,
And theſe the ſhowers to bring it on: be cheerfull.

Octa. Sir,looke well to my Husbands houſe: and
Cæſar. What *Octauia*?
Octa. Ile tell you in your eare.
Ant. Her tongue will not obey her heart,nor can
Her heart informe her tougue.
The Swannes downe feather
That ſtands vpon the Swell at the of full Tide:
And neither way inclines.
Eno. Will *Cæſar* weepe?
Agr. He ha's a cloud in's face.
Eno. He were the worſe for that were he a Horſe ſo is he being a man.
Agri. Why *Enobarbus*:
When *Anthony* found *Iulius Cæſar* dead,
He cried almoſt to roaring: And he wept,
When at Phillippi he found *Brutus* ſlaine.
Eno. That year indeed,he was trobled with a rume,
What willingly he did confound,he wail'd,
Beleeu't till I weepe too.
Cæſar. No ſweet *Octauia*,
You ſhall heare from me ſtill: the time ſhall not
Out-go my thinking on you.
Ant. Come Sir,come,
Ile wraſtle with you in my ſtrength of loue,
Looke heere I haue you,thus I let you go,
And giue you to the Gods.
Cæſar. Adieu,be happy.
Lep. Let all the number of the Starres giue light
To thy faire way.
Cæſar. Farewell,farewell. *Kiſſes Octauia.*
Ant. Farewell. *Trumpets ſound. Exeunt.*

Enter Cleopatra,Charmian,Iras,and Alexas.

Cleo. Where is the Fellow?
Alex. Halfe afeard to come.
Cleo. Go too,go too: Come hither Sir.
Enter the Meſſenger as before.
Alex. Good Maieſtie: *Herod* of Iury dare not looke vpon you,but when you are well pleas'd.
Cleo. That *Herods* head, Ile haue: but how? When *Anthony* is gone,through whom I might commaund it:
Come thou neere.
Meſ. Moſt gratious Maieſtie.
Cleo Did'ſt thou behold *Octauia*?
Meſ. I dread Queene.
Cleo. Where?
Meſ. Madam in Rome, I lookt her in the face: and ſaw her led betweene her Brother, and *Marke Anthony.*
Cleo. Is ſhe as tall as me?
Meſ. She is not Madam.
Cleo. Didſt heare her ſpeake?
Is ſhe ſhrill tongu'd or low?
Meſ. Madam,I heard her ſpeake,ſhe is low voic'd.
Cleo. That's not ſo good: he cannot like her long.
Char. Like her? Oh *Iſis*: 'tis impoſſible.
Cleo. I thinke ſo *Charmian*: dull of tongue, & dwarfiſh
What Maieſtie is in her gate,remember
If ere thou look'ſt on Maieſtie.
Meſ. She creepes:her motion,& her ſtation are as one.
She ſhewes a body,rather then a life,
A Statue,then a Breather.
Cleo. Is this certaine?
Meſ. Or I haue no obſeruance.
Cha. Three in Egypt cannot make better note.
Cleo. He's very knowing,I do perceiu't,
There's nothing in her yet.
The

Proof-page of Antony and Cleopatra from the First Folio (1623), sig. xxo[v]. It represents the uncorrected state of the page and shows the proof-reader's marks indicating corrections. All but two of the corrections here marked were duly made in the corrected state.

Shakespeare's time was not completely without system, the spelling of books was still largely determined by the printer's individual habits and the amount of trouble he took over his work. Thus the Folio, the type of which was set by several different compositors, shows considerable variations in this respect. In an Elizabethan printer's shop the proofs were read and corrected page by page while printing was in progress. As not all the uncorrected pages were eliminated, and as the proof-corrections to a particular page were sometimes made several times while the edition was being printed, no two copies of the First Folio are identical. Every copy is a mixture of uncorrected and more or less carefully proof-read pages. Mistakes could also happen when later changes to the text made it necessary for the printer to replace a single leaf (consisting, of course, of two printed pages), with a newly-printed leaf. Some copies of the Folio still have the old leaf or the old and new leaves together. Such mistakes can sometimes throw interesting light on changes that were made for religious, political or even purely literary reasons.

A sixteenth-century printing shop. From Stephen Batman, *The Doom Warning All Men to the Judgement* (1581). The printing press here shown, in all essentials typical of presses used down to the end of the eighteenth century, is being worked at "full press" (i.e. with two men), one man (right) removing from the tympan a sheet just printed off, the other inking the type-bed with the ink-balls, preparatory to the next "pull". Note (left) the "platten" (half the size of a sheet), fastened flexibly at the lower end of the large screw spindle, which, when the carriage was slid back under it, was brought down evenly and firmly on the type-bed by a strong pull of the "bar" to make the impression. In the foreground arc two "piles", one of sheets already printed off in the press-run, the other of sheets still waiting to be "impressed". In the rear of the shop a compositor (right), sitting before a "case" of type, is seen setting from "copy", which is held in a copy-holder to his left. Opposite him, another compositor is either making press-corrections or setting type.

Before the task of type-setting could begin the printer had to guess how much of the manuscript would fill each of the 12 pages of 3 folio sheets, which were printed together and sewn together when the book came to be bound. As two of the folded sheets had to be put inside the remaining sheet the order of the 12 pages was rather complicated. This made it necessary for the printer to work out in advance how many lines of the manuscript were needed to fill 12 folio pages. If he guessed wrongly and ran out of space he had to condense the text a little, either by leaving something out or by turning verse into prose.

→ **emendation** [ˌi:men'deɪʃən] the change made when a mistake in a text is corrected

It was only after careful work of several generations of scholars that sources of error such as these were identified and a more correct text of Shakespeare established.

From one Folio edition of Shakespeare to the next the editors showed a growing tendency to correct what they thought to be errors made by their predecessors and to modernize the spelling, vocabulary and grammar. Unfortunately they often introduced new errors and unnecessary improvements. The Second Folio (1632) contained no fewer than 1,679 emendations in the 36 plays reprinted from the First Folio. About 800 of these corrections, however, were justified and are included in modern editions of Shakespeare's works. The first issue of the Third Folio (1663) also contained 36 plays. The second issue (1664) included PERICLES and six other plays which were then thought to be by Shakespeare. The Fourth Folio (1685) was a reprint of the 43 plays of the second issue of the Third Folio, but contained 751 changes or emendations of its own. Though this was perhaps the worst of the four Folios it has come to be regarded as historically interesting, as one of the several 17th-century attempts to create a reliable and useful edition of Shakespeare's plays.

5.5.2. A few important later editions

Many of the 18th and 19th century editors from Rowe to Malone made serious attempts to provide a reliable text of Shakespeare, comparing as many different readings from the early editions as they could and trying to fix upon the best. Nevertheless, "they worked by hit-or-miss systems and substituted their own (often excellent) tastes for critical principles."[15] Perhaps only Edward Capell occupies a special position among them. He was the first to publish critical notes on the text, listing variant readings for all earlier editions, trying to determine the relative authority of the early editions, especially the Quartos.

Between 1854 and 1861 a two-volume Shakespeare came out under the editorship of the German scholar Nikolaus Delius. The text he established is still considered to be of value today. It was used by F. J. Furnivall in his popular one-volume "Leopold Shakespeare" of 1877, dedicated to Prince Leopold, duke of Albany.

Between 1863 and 1866 W. G. Clark, J. Glover and W. A. Wright published the "Cambridge Shakespeare", the most important 19th-century critical edition of Shakespeare's plays. Here, too, were listed the variants and emendations from earlier editions. For a long time it was the stand-

→ **Rowe** [rəʊ] Nicholas (1674–1718) English poet and playwright and the first authoritative biographer of Shakespeare; brought out the first critical edition of Shakespeare's work
→ **Malone** [mə'ləʊn], Edmund (1741–1812) critic, wrote the first serious study of the chronology of the poet's plays
→ **Capell** ['keɪpəl], Edward (1713–1781) the first to adopt the principle that any edition of Shakespeare should be based on the "good" Quartos and the First Folio
→ **Delius** ['di:ljəs], Nikolaus (1813–1888) German scholar, wrote a Shakespeare dictionary
→ **Furnivall** ['fɜ:nɪvəl], Frederic James (1825–1910): founder of the New Shakespeare Society
→ **Clark** [kla:k], William George (1821–1878)
→ **Wright** [raɪt], William Aldis (1836?–1914)

History of a play manuscript in Shakespeare's time

(An attempt at illustrating and supplementing the account given by G. B. Harrison in his chapter on "Editing Shakespeare", p. 193 ff.)

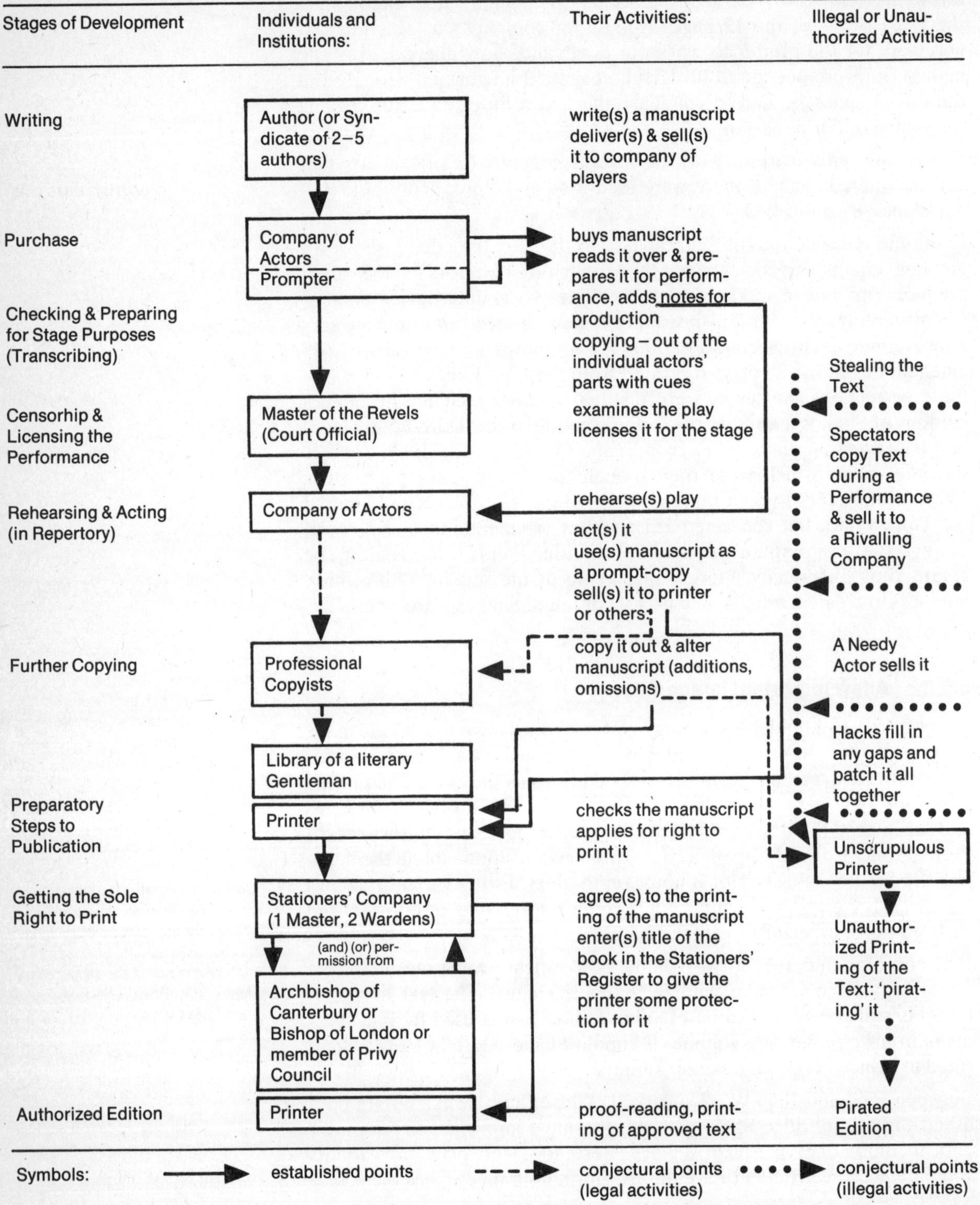

ard text. The Cambridge editors also published a one-volume Shakespeare, "The Globe Edition" (1866), which won considerable popularity and has remained the standard for line numbering.

"The Arden Shakespeare", published under the editorship of W. J. Craig and R. H. Case between 1899 and 1924, was another distinguished scholarly edition, with detailed critical notes, emendations and variants from earlier editions. It has been completely re-edited as "The New Arden Shakespeare" since 1951 under the general editorship of U. Ellis-Fermor, H. F. Brooks and others. Like the Arden, the "New Cambridge" edition (Sir Arthur Quiller-Couch and J. Dover Wilson, 1921 onwards) devotes one volume to each play, providing a text with as few emendations as possible and never losing sight of the First Folio readings.

The "New Variorum" edition continues the tradition established by three 19th century variorum editions, quoting and discussing notes and comments by many different editors, scholars and critics (cum notis variorum, i.e. 'with notes from various hands') and also giving textual variants. The "New Variorum" began with the publication of H. H. Furness's edition of ROMEO AND JULIET in 1871. This edition has been in progress for more than 100 years; 27 volumes, each of them containing one of Shakespeare's plays, had been published by 1955. The volumes edited since 1936 are considered to be most valuable.

In 1974 "The Riverside Shakespeare" was published under the textual editorship of G. Blakemore Evans. This American one-volume edition of Shakespeare's work was printed for the general reading public and the scholars as well, offering them a completely re-edited text whose spelling and punctuation are mostly modern though they sometimes reflect Elizabethan pronunciation and speech rhythm.

Peter Alexander's one-volume edition of the "Complete Works" (1951) is the most satisfactory complete text of Shakespeare we have, and is in fact the standard reference text among scholars and critics.

In the last forty years there have also been many excellent paperback editions, each filling many volumes. These include G. H. Harrison's old "Penguin Shakespeare", the "Signet Classic Shakespeare" (general editor Sylvan Barnet) and "The New Penguin Shakespeare" (general editor T. B. B. Spencer). A useful school edition for those whose first language is not English is the "New Swan Shakespeare" (general editor Bernard Lott).

→ **Craig** [kreɪg]
→ **scholarly** ['skɒləli] based on serious academic study
→ **Ellis-Fermor** ['elis'fɜʳːmɔːr] Una
→ **Brooks** [ʊ]
→ **Quiller-Couch** [ˌkwilə'kʊːtʃ], Sir Arthur T. (1863–1944) novelist
→ **Wilson**, John Dover (1881–1969)
→ **rhythm** ['rɪðəm]
→ **Alexander** [ˌæligzaːndəʳ], Peter (1894–)
→ **reference** ['refərəns] (here) looked at for information
→ **Harrison** G. B. (1894–)
→ Sylvan **Barnett** ['sɪlvən 'baːnɪt]
→ **Lott** [ɒ], B.

15 J. Crow, "Textual Criticism", in *Encyclopaedia Britannica*, ed. in chief Harry S. Ashmore, Chicago, London, Toronto, 1961, vol. 20, p. 455.

6. The Elizabethan Age

6.1. The Italian Renaissance

"If Shakespeare's plays and poems are the monument of a remarkable genius, they are also the monument of a remarkable age."[16] This "remarkable age" was the Renaissance, which began in northern Italy in the 13th century and which, in the course of the next 300 years, spread over the whole of Europe. The term "renaissance", which the English borrowed from the French, means "rebirth" and was originally used by Italian writers – Giorgio Vasari spoke of "la rinascita" in 1550 – to convey two components of the same idea. First of all, it represented a complete break with the 1000 years which went before it, in which intellectual activity appeared to be dead. Secondly, it was seen as a revival of ancient Roman, and also Greek, civilization and culture; the architecture of the Romans and Greeks was studied, their statues were copied and their texts were collected and interpreted.

The period of history before the Renaissance, that is, between the decline of the Roman Empire and the rise of Christianity in Europe up to the Middle Ages with the emergence of the Italian city-states is still referred to as the "Dark Ages", a time about which little is known, a time in which human creativity and endeavour seem to have been at a standstill. Though this conception may not be accurate, it must be said that the Church, the most powerful force in the community, sometimes showed little interest in developing the intellectual faculties of its followers. Learning, as well as literacy, was often a privilege of the clergy. Early manuscripts were copied, but sometimes jealously guarded in the libraries of monasteries or cathedrals. The Renaissance was a movement often directed against the overwhelming domination of the Church and against the privileges of the clergy. Literacy spread among the laity, texts were copied, and later printed, so that more and more people were able to study them. The study of language and rhetoric spread, not only because it was essential for the translation and interpretation of old texts but also because of the conviction of Renaissance scholars that they were carrying on the work of civilization which the Greeks and Romans had started.

Emphasis was placed on the dignity of man (in contrast to the feudal idea of man as a dependent and therefore unfree being) and on the question of how dignity was to be achieved. The Humanists felt that they had found the answer to this question. They believed that the only way to dignity was through knowledge and advocated the *studia humanitatis*, a curriculum which they adapted from the Romans and which included among other things grammar, rhetoric, poetry and philosophy. The study of nature and its laws was also encouraged and, in the course of time, important new ideas on man, the state and the universe emerged. Most important was man's steady shift towards the centre of the universe; by learning and exploring, man had come to dominate nature and from this point onwards he was able to determine his own fate and exercise his own free will. Hand in hand with this spiritual and intellectual development,

→ **Vasari** [va'za:ri], Giorgio (1511–1574) Italian painter, architect, and art historian
→ **to convey** carry (from one place to another); (here) to communicate
→ **revival** new interest (in s.th. that was out of fashion)
→ **emergence** [ɪ'mɜ:dʒəns] appearance; rise (in status or importance)
→ **endeavour** [ɪn'devəʳ] activity; effort
→ **faculties** powers; ability
→ **literacy** ability to read and write
→ **clergy** all the religious officials who are authorized to hold a church service
→ **overwhelming** very great; überwältigend
→ **laity** ['leɪəti] people who have no office in the church (opposite of clergy)
→ **dignity** true worth and nobleness; (here) high position; Würde
→ **to advocate** to support and speak in favour of s.th.
→ **steady** [e] constant
→ **shift** movement; change of place

great advances were made in the sciences. A new orientation in astronomy helped to shatter the harmony between religious beliefs on the one hand and scientific knowledge on the other. The theory that the earth was the centre of the universe was challenged by Copernicus in 1543, by Kepler in 1609 and by Galilei in 1610. Although most people remained faithful to Ptolemy's geocentric theory of the universe, there was, by Shakespeare's time, a small group of scientists which had begun to adopt the Copernican view.

The Renaissance was an age of invention, discovery and exploration and perhaps the spirit of the age is best shown in the Voyages of Discovery. Christopher Columbus reached America in 1492, Vasco da Gama sailed round the Cape of Good Hope to India in 1498 and during the next century a host of Spanish, Portuguese and English sailors set off to explore the seas. The reasons behind these voyages and the circumstances under which they were undertaken go a long way towards explaining what the Renaissance was. First of all, the Renaissance was an age in which man began to widen the horizons of his universe; the voyages of discovery were the geographical expression of this. Secondly, the Renaissance was an age of scientific invention and one of the most important inventions – although it had already been known to the Chinese for centuries – was the mariner's compass which allowed sailors to venture out into the open sea instead of following the coastline as they had done until then. Thirdly, the Renaissance was an age of growing trade between sovereign states; riches, until then unknown in Europe, were brought back from the Near and Far East and from the New World, as America was known at first. The city-states of northern Italy were the first to experience the new wealth (and, along with it, the power) which resulted from trade with the Near East. Capital was accumulated, banks were established and large-scale trading developed; this was the dawn of the Capitalist era. The circle is now full-drawn. Since the profits made from trade with the Near East were so great that not all the money was needed for re-investment in trade, money was also available for the arts and science.

The Renaissance, then, was the start of a new period of history; it was the beginning of our 'Modern Age'. Profound changes took place in the economic system which, in turn, led to new developments not only in politics and diplomacy but also in culture and the arts. By the early 16th century, the Renaissance had reached its climax and was nearing its end in Italy, the country of its birth. In England, however, it had only just begun and it was to have its greatest influence there in Shakespeare's time.

→ **to shatter** to break, destroy
→ **to challenge** ['tʃæləndʒ]: (here) to call into question
→ **Ptolemy** ['tɒlɪmɪ] Greek astronomer, mathematician, and geographer of second century A.D.; resident in Alexandria
→ **mariner** ['mærənəʳ] sailor
→ **to venture out** to go out although there is a risk of danger
→ **available** able to be got or obtained

16 L. G. Salingar, "The Elizabethan Renaissance", in *The Pelican Guide to English Literature: The Age of Shakespeare*, ed. B. Ford. Harmondsworth: Penguin Books Ltd. 1962, repr., p. 51.

6.2. The Renaissance in England

The year 1485 is generally regarded as the beginning of the Renaissance in England. This was an important year in England's history since it marked the end of a long and bloody civil war in which two rival branches of the Plantagenet family, the House of Lancaster and the House of York, had fought each other for the English throne. The Wars of the Roses, as they were called (because of the emblems of each House – the red rose of Lancashire and the white rose of York), ended with the defeat of Richard III, of the house of York, at the battle of Bosworth Field. The new king, Henry VII, was the first of a new line, or dynasty, of English sovereigns known as the Tudors, who were to reign until 1603 when the last Tudor queen, Elizabeth I, died. The period of Tudor rule is characterized by the growing importance of the monarch and the corresponding decline in the status of the local leader, the baron. This was not only due to the increase in the power of the monarch as a result of the introduction of gunpowder into Europe in the 12th century and the subsequent development of weapons such as cannons which were for a long time the prerogative of the monarch. It also reflected a growing spirit of nationalism in western Europe in which the citizens of a town like London began to regard themselves not only as citizens of London but also as Englishmen. In addition, many influential local leaders had been killed in the Wars of the Roses.

→ **corresponding** accompanying; developing in a similar way (entsprechend)
→ **gunpowder** explosive substance for firing guns, cannons, etc.
→ **subsequent** ['sʌbsɪkwənt] following (usually as a result)
→ **weapon** [e] instrument used in a fight or war (gun, sword, etc.)
→ **prerogative** [prɪ'rɒgətɪv] exclusive right

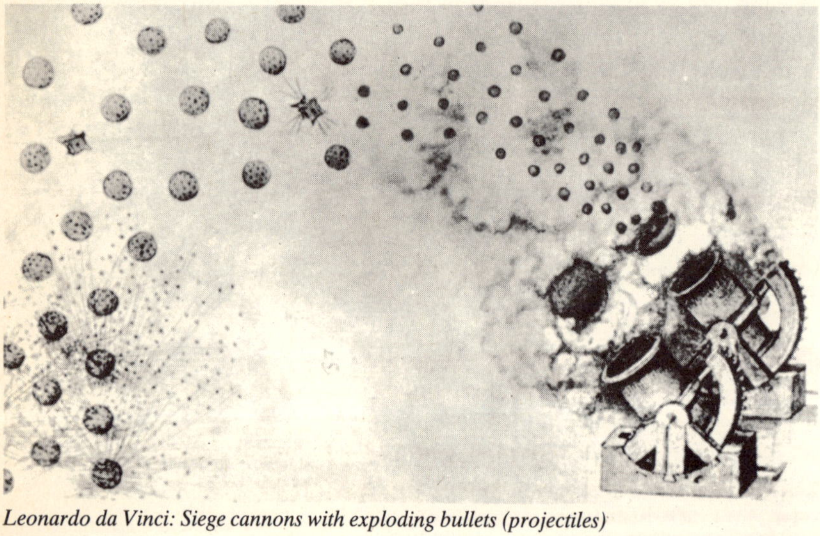

Leonardo da Vinci: Siege cannons with exploding bullets (projectiles)

The use of the cannon and the growing spirit of nationalism are only two of the many changes which took place at the dawn of the "Modern Age" – the Renaissance – which came to England later than it did to other parts of Europe. First of all, England was an island: it had its own traditions and was not easily influenced, politically as well as culturally, as countries on the European continent. It was also furthest away from the city-states of northern Italy, where the Renaissance began. Secondly, the civil war, which had lasted for thirty years, had caused a considerable amount of destruction and had stopped all progress in the social, political and economic development of the country.

Under the Tudor monarchs, England experienced the same changes that had taken place in other European countries. The reorganization of the economic system, characterized by large-scale trading at home and abroad as well as by the rise of banking houses, brought forth a new class which competed, more and more successfully as time went on, with the old aristocracy for the favour of the monarch. Increasingly, court officials and officials of state were chosen from the ranks of the new bourgeoisie and it was this class which set new standards in education and learning. Grammar schools and colleges were founded, notably at Oxford and Cambridge, and the role of the teacher, the philosopher and the scientist grew as the influence of the Church became weaker.

It is no coincidence that the Reformation began during this period. The study of ancient Roman and Greek authors, the progress of science and the critical spirit of the new age all helped to weaken the authority of the Church of Rome. At the same time, the power of the monarch was increasing and the more his power grew, the less desire he had to share it, especially with a foreigner, as the Pope in Rome was. The monarch claimed the right to choose the highest officials of the church, the bishops, himself, although it must be added that the monarch envied not only the influence of the Church but also its immense wealth. The final break with Rome in 1534 under Henry VIII, who reigned from 1509 to 1547, saw the beginning of a long period of religious and social unrest which divided the nation, but which finally resulted in the strengthening of the Church of England (the Anglican Church) under Elizabeth I (1558–1603). This did not mean, however, that the conflict with Rome was over. Many attempts were made, both diplomatically and militarily, to win England back to Roman Catholicism. The most notable of these was the Armada, a fleet of Spanish ships which set sail in 1588 to conquer England. The defeat by Elizabeth's Royal Navy was a major event in English history; not only did it serve to encourage the spirit of national pride among Englishmen, but it also established England as one of the most powerful countries in the world at that time.

→ **large-scale** in great numbers or quantities
→ **trading** buying and selling for a profit
→ **to compete** [kəm'pi:t] to be rivals with others (in sport, trade, etc.)
→ **notably** worthy of attention
→ **coincidence** [kəʊ'ɪnsɪdəns] happening by chance of two unconnected events at the same time (Zufall)
→ **to envy** ['envi] to desire strongly what another person has and to feel discontented that one has not got it

Inquisition in England under Mary Tudor (1553–58). She was fanatically Catholic (daughter of Henry VIII's Spanish wife Catherine of Aragon and married to the Spanish king Philip II) and brutally tried to restore Catholicism in England (hence 'Bloody Mary'). – The above picture on a contemporary pamphlet shows leaders of the Protestant Party being publicly burned at the stake in Newbury (1556).

The great naval battle of 1588 when the Spanish Armada was destroyed. King Philip II of Spain rigged up the Armada in order to put an end to the piracy of English adventurers on the Spanish merchant fleet (bringing home to Spain the South American riches). – Queen Elizabeth protected these activities and, in return, profited from the prizes, thus having her share in the Spanish colonies' wealth.

The Armadas – for there were more than the one just mentioned in 1588 – were not sent to conquer England for religious reasons alone. England and Spain, as well as being religious rivals after the Reformation, were also rivals in trade. The centre of economic and political activity was gradually shifting from central Europe and northern Italy to the Atlantic coast, from Spain and Portugal in the south to England and the Netherlands in the north. This shift was closely connected with foreign trade, whose importance was rapidly increasing in the new economic system which was developing in the countries of western Europe. Since the Turks were blockading the traditional overland routes to India and China, it was necessary to find other ways of reaching these countries and sailors were encouraged to explore the seas for new routes to the Far East. These voyages resulted in the discovery of America by Christopher Columbus in 1492 and of a sea route to India around the Cape of Good Hope by Vasco da Gama six years later. England was well situated geographically to take part in the exploration of the seas and John Cabot, who discovered Labrador in 1498 while searching for a north-west passage to China, was the first of a long line of famous Elizabethan sailors who, within a century, were to make England a major sea power.

The rise of capitalism increased the income of the monarch and brought prosperity to the new class of merchants and to a host of professional people, such as teachers and doctors, whom they supported. However, it also had negative effects. The competitive and calculating spirit created by the new system was often without regard for human relations and disrupted the values and social order of feudalism. The quest for profit

→ **to shift** to move from one place to another
→ **host** [həʊst] large number
→ **to disrupt** to throw into disorder
→ **quest** search
→ **in kind** (of payment) using goods or natural products rather than money
→ **to promote** to support, encourage (here: durchsetzen)

overturned the agrarian structure of medieval society and replaced the concept of common interests by one of promoting personal interests. As a result of foreign trade and piracy, large quantities of Spanish gold and silver entered Elizabethan England. This had the effect of lowering the value of English money which, in turn, resulted in sharply increased prices not only for manufactured goods but also for basic products such as food. The old order was at an end. Feudalism was based on the ownership of land and on the relationship between the landlord, the owner of the land, and the tenant, who farmed the land and paid a rent to the landlord for the use of the land. For centuries this rent had often been paid in kind; that is, by giving the landlord a portion of the produce which he farmed and by performing certain duties such as serving as a soldier if his landlord needed men either to protect his territory or to reinforce his claim on the territory of others. Payment in money, however, gradually superseded payment in kind. When, therefore, English currency started to lose much of its value, landlords were faced with a sharp drop in their standard of living and began looking for ways of increasing their income. One obvious method was to put up the rents which their tenants had to pay; another was connected with the growing importance of cloth at that time. It was soon more profitable to raise sheep for the wool, from which cloth was made in those days, than to grow corn, and many landlords proceeded to fence in not only their own fields but also the common grassland of their villages and turning them into pastures for sheep. These two developments meant disaster for a large section of the population who lived on the land. Many tenants could not afford the new rents and were forced to leave their farms, and the enclosure movement, the fencing in of the village commons, put many labourers out of work. Thousands of people turned to the roads, swelling the numbers of the vagabonds and beggars, who were already a serious problem for the authorities. Only gradually did reforms take place and it was not until Shakespeare's time that, in theory at least, the old and the sick were taken care of by the communities and the able-bodied poor were put to work.

The standard of living of the new bourgeoisie was steadily rising, thus creating a climate favourable for the development of the Renaissance in England. The great upheaval in the economic and social system was reflected in the cultural life of the country and innovations were made in the arts, in education and the sciences, and in language and communication. As far as the latter is concerned, the Renaissance in England started in 1476 when William Caxton set up his printing press at Westminster. In the following 14 years Caxton published about 80 books, many of them translations of foreign works which helped to spread new, often humanist, ideas from abroad. In his work Caxton soon became aware of the difficulties of a language which had not been fixed in print and sought to establish standards of spelling, vocabulary and grammar of the English language. He had to choose "bytwene playn, rude & curyous"[17] terms and contributed a great deal towards the standardization of English. In his own prose Caxton strove to improve his language, and used the contemporary speech of the people of London, thus helping to spread the use of London English far beyond the boundaries of the city.

→ **to reinforce** [ˌri:ɪn'fɔ:s] to make stronger
→ **to supersede** [ˌsu:pə'si:d] to replace, especially as an improvement on s.th.
→ **currency** money (coins and notes) in use in a country
→ **to proceed** to begin
→ **pasture** ['pa:stʃə^r] grassland for sheep, cows, etc.
→ **upheaval** [ʌp'hi:vəl] great (social) change
→ **innovation** s.th. completely new which is introduced
→ **the latter** [æ] the last named or mentioned
→ **to strive** strove, striven to work hard for s.th.; to make great efforts
→ **comtemporary** [kən'tempərəri] of that time; of the period of time which is being discussed

England already had a strongly-developed, native, literary tradition which had earlier assimilated foreign influences without losing its own peculiarities and, in the same way, it adapted the new ideas of the Renaissance without loss of its native strength. Characters of ancient Roman and Greek mythology, events which had happened centuries before, place names of the Mediterranean world – all these entered the literature, and in particular the drama, of England without submerging local traditions. The language, too, underwent considerable change; under the influence of humanist studies at schools and colleges England acquired a vast amount of new words, reflecting the new ideas which were being absorbed, and, in addition, competition between poets as well as between playwrights encouraged the development of rhetoric and eloquent speech. Drama became an increasingly popular form of entertainment, attracting an audience which was trained to listen to the spoken tongue rather than to read language in print. In fact it can be said that, in the field of literature, the Renaissance in England reached its zenith with Elizabethan drama and in particular with the plays of Shakespeare.

→ **to submerge** [səb'mɜːdʒ] to cover over (originally with water)
→ **to absorb** [əb'sɔːb] to take in, assimilate
→ **eloquent** ['eləkwənt] skilful in the use of language; elegant in style

17 A. C. Baugh, *A History of the English Language*, London: Routlege & Kegan Paul Ltd., 1963, 2nd ed., repr., p. 236.

6.3. The Elizabethan view of the world

6.3.1. Some general concepts

Although the Elizabethan age was one of great social and cultural change, Shakespeare's contemporaries had a view of the world which was still strongly influenced by medieval tradition and still deeply rooted in the teachings of the Christian Church. Even Renaissance ideas about the structure of the universe taken from ancient Greek philosophers were adapted to the beliefs of the Church.

According to these beliefs, God had created the universe and everything in it; out of chaos He had established Order and Unity and had bound all lifeless and living things together in a system in which each object and being had its rightful place in nature, according to its rank and usefulness. Medieval man was well aware of this Order and of the necessity of keeping it at all costs. He was also very well aware of his own place in the universe and of his duty to obey the laws of nature as well as those of God. In order to fulfil this duty man was obliged to love and worship God and, what is more, to learn about Him by studying his Book of Books (the Bible) and by contemplating His creation (the Book of Nature).

These beliefs were still valid in the age of the Renaissance but the form of study and contemplation gradually changed and became more active. Man had to go out and explore the world which God had given to him. It was man's birthright to govern the world and, in order to do so, he made use of the "arts" which he had developed through the years – astronomy, logic, rhetoric and poetry, to name but a few. His commercial and political activities were in harmony with the laws of nature since it was trade that was pushing back the frontiers of the world.

→ **chaos** ['keɪ–ɒs] a state of complete disorder and confusion –
→ **rank** degree of value and importance
→ **to contemplate** to think deeply about s.th.
→ **valid** (of a reason) having a strong firm base

6.3.2. Structure and composition of the Elizabethan universe

In Shakespeare's age people still believed that the Earth was at the centre of a system of vast circles drawn by the Moon, Sun, and Moving Stars (i.e. the planets). This was the so-called geo-centric universe. Above the earth and its region which extended up to the Moon's sphere (i.e. the "sublunar world") and surrounding it from all sides was the cosmos, the ordered universal world. Its concentric circles of varying size marked the eight paths of the stars around the Earth: there were the planets such as the Moon, Mercury, Venus, the Sun, Mars, Jupiter, Saturn, and the circular band of the Fixed Stars, the so-called Firmament or Zodiac (from the late Greek *zôdion*: 'sculptured figure of a little animal'). The circle of the Zodiac was divided into 12 parts, each part consisting of a group of Fixed Stars (i.e. stars appearing to have no movement of their own). They were believed to influence the lives of inferior beings in the "sublunar world" and were named after animals with which they shared certain characteristics: e.g. Aries, Taurus, Gemini, Cancer, Leo, etc. The eight concentric circles of the planets from the Moon to Saturn and the Zodiac were thought to be transparent bodies, so-called spheres which revolved at different speeds. The number of spheres that made up the universe could be nine or eleven, for a Crystallinum or even two such crystalline spheres could be added to the existing eight spheres. The Crystallinum extended outside the Zodiac (or Firmament). People thought that it influenced the date of those two periods of the year when day and night are of equal length. A further and outermost sphere, surrounding the Crystallinum, was regarded as the border of the universe. It was the master sphere, the *primum mobile*. Revolving from west to east once in every 24 hours, it set the planetary spheres in motion from east to west. Through the movements of the planets it also influenced movement and change on Earth.

→ **sublunar** [sʌb'luːnəʳ] belonging to the region below the Moon's sphere
→ **Mercury** ['mɜːkjuri]
→ **Venus** ['viːnəs]
→ **Mars** [maːz]
→ **Jupiter** ['dʒuːpɪtəʳ]
→ **Saturn** ['sætən]
→ **Zodiac** ['zəʊdiæk]
→ **crystallinum** [ˌkrɪstə'laɪnəm]
→ **crystalline** ['krɪstəlaɪn] of or like crystal

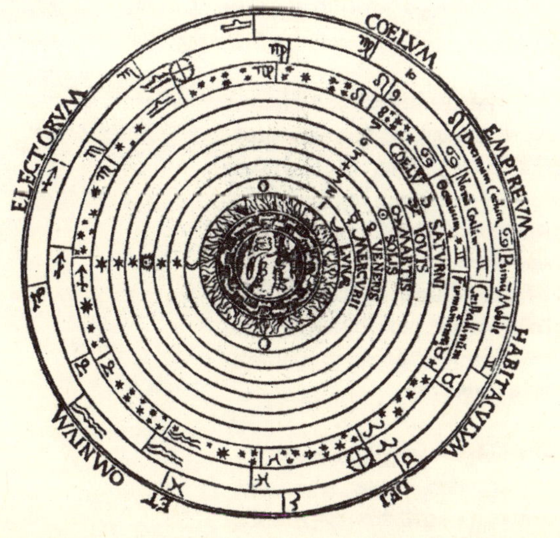

Plan of the Universe by Peter Apian, a sixteenth-century astronomer. Note that outside the primum mobile he assumes there is a static heaven, the abode of God and the elect.

Outside the nine or eleven spheres of the created universe was Heaven, the eternal Empyreum (also Empireum; from the Greek *èmpýrios:* 'fiery, radiating light'). It was here that God, the angels and the souls of the blessed were believed to be. From here God's angels acted as His messengers and as man's guardians, and they also regulated the movement of the different planetary spheres. This vast system of revolving and transparent bodies was called the Aethereum (from the Greek *aíthein:* 'to burn'). Some scholars believed that the Aethereum was filled with Aether, a fifth element which was purer than earth, water, air, and fire – the four elements of which the universe was composed – and which was the substance of the stars and their spheres. Others believed that the Aethereum was made up of a more perfect and purer form of the elements, especially of air and fire. As the transparent spheres of the different planets revolved at different speeds, the friction they caused created the heavenly music of the spheres which man, after Adam's fall, had no longer been able to perceive.

The innermost and central part of the universe, which extended below the Moon's sphere, belonged to the four elements, the Earth, its world of created objects and, above all, to man and his social and political world. When Adam succumbed to the Devil's temptation in Paradise, this sublunar region was sharply divided from the beauty, constancy and harmony of the eternal Aethereum. With this first act of disobedience against God man disturbed the original harmony and peace of his part of the universe. God punished him by sending disorder, illness, death and destruction into the sublunar world, without however taking away all of its order and beauty. He also left man some of his original willpower and reason, thus enabling him to obey His commandments and to study the Bible and the Book of Nature. Together with all created beings sinful man became subject to change, decay and death. Man's life, too, was largely dependent on external fate: either on the unjust rule of a wilful female power called Fortune or on the influence of the moon and stars which varied according to the constellations of good or evil stars.

The four elements of earth, water, air and fire, the building material of the whole universe, were perfectly mixed above the Moon's sphere; they became purer the nearer they were to God's Empyreum. Below the Moon, however, – because of Adam's fall – they were to be found in different mixtures of inferior quality; the closer the elements or their mixtures came to the centre of the universe, the rawer, heavier and impurer they became. Hell and the place of the damned souls were believed to be deep down in the Earth, which after Adam's fall had become a kind of vast underground storeroom for worthless or ruined substances and for waste material from the whole universe.

This was a pessimistic view of man and his world. It must, however, be set against Renaissance man's readiness to admire and enjoy what was left of the original beauty and order of the universe and his hope of a better life to come if man did not fail in his worship of and obedience towards God the Almighty.

→ **Empyreum** [ˌempɪˈrɪəm]
→ **Aethereum** [iːθəˈrɪəm]
→ **Aether** [ˈiːθəʳ]
→ **fall** a change to a life of sin from a life of goodness
→ **to succumb** [səˈkʌm] to yield
→ **wilful** having or showing the intention of doing what one likes, in spite of other people

The old view of the world in the first Luther-Bible (printed 1534 in Wittenberg by Hans Luft).

6.3.3. Nature, creation and man

Renaissance man's twofold view of creation which combined "extremes of optimism and pessimism"[18] also included Nature who was regarded as both good and evil. As part of God's creation, spoilt by Adam's original sin, Nature not only gave life and form to the objects of the created world, but also allowed decay and destruction. After Adam's fall she was determined to follow her own wishes, although she did not remove all signs of God's will and order. She was considered to be God's instrument, an intelligent and fertile female being who was active in every corner of the created universe. Placed below the angels and above man, Nature acted according to her own rules (the law of Nature), carrying out God's will without being conscious of doing so. Nature was thus regarded as a visible expression of God's intentions.

As a creative force Nature owned regions where her order was constantly threatened by chaos and disorder. Elizabethan man regarded this disorder as a kind of universal anarchy which would succeed in disturbing and destroying the universe and man's political world alike if God did not preserve Nature and her influence, even though occasional disturbances were inevitable. Such temporary disturbances in Nature's rule occurred on the different levels of Creation: cosmic disorder created by adverse constellations of the stars could be accompanied by a war among the elements (e.g. a thunderstorm) or by animals defying Nature's order (e.g. when a falcon was attacked by an owl, a weaker and less noble bird). Events such as these may follow the death of kings, as a warning or a sign of a coming civil war within the state. Political unrest in its turn could have been caused by disorder within the soul or little world (i.e. microcosm) of an ambitious general or a powerful prince.

Nature ruled over three levels of Creation: firstly the Moving and Fixed Stars in the Aethereum; secondly, the sphere below the Moon, the region of the Earth with its objects, plants and animals and, finally, man's social and political world. The law of Nature bound everything which God had created into a hierarchy of lifeless and living things. This hierarchy can be imagined as a Chain of Beings, the traditional idea of the Elizabethans, or as a great ladder with many rungs; at the bottom of the ladder were lifeless things like stones or metals (gold, of course, ranking above iron). Higher up came plants and trees (the oak, being the sturdiest, occupied the highest rung among these) and after them, animals, among which an ox, for example, held a higher place than a cat. Then came man in varying degrees from kings to paupers and, above man, the angels. On the highest rung of the ladder God watched over his creation from Heaven, situated outside the universe he had created. Degree established the different positions of created beings, binding them together within a unity and hierarchy: degree helped Nature to order the variety of God's creatures, preventing them from falling back into chaos: degree established harmony, mutual assistance and dependence among creatures.

Shakespeare's contemporaries further believed in a rather complicated system of correspondences among the different levels of creation. Perhaps the best example of this is the correspondence between the

→ **adverse** ['ædvɜːs] opposing
→ **falcon** ['fɔːlkən] Falke
→ **owl** [aʊl] Eule
→ **microcosm** ['maɪkrəʊkɒzəm]
→ **hierarchy** ['haɪərɑːki] the organization of a system into higher and lower ranks
→ **rung** [ʌ] one of the cross-bars that form the steps of a ladder
→ **degree** (here) rank or place in a hierarchy
→ **pauper** [ɔː] a person who is very poor

microcosm of man's soul and the macrocosm of the universe, which was based on a great many similarities. The Sun, for instance, was in the midst of the Aethereum giving the planets light and power much in the same way as the heart in the midst of man's body acted in a corresponding way. Man's head resembled the noblest stars as it, too, was placed highest in its own sphere. Man's passions were compared to earthquakes and storms in nature. Man's world of government and the universe were linked together and illustrated by countless analogies. God, the Sun, king and reason all had similar ruling functions whereas the passions within man's microcosm were compared to disordered crowds of noisy people. Correspondences were also to be found in Nature's creatures. Thus the king's ruling power and position within the state was compared to the rank of the eagle among the birds or to the position of the lion among the animals living on land. Countless similar analogies served to recall the idea of order and harmony underlying the cosmic, the natural, and the political patterns of Nature's world which he saw constantly challenged by change and development.

The hierarchical patterns of Nature's cosmological order among the planets and of her natural order among the creatures on earth reflected the political order within the third of Nature's regions, man's world of government. Here, too, Nature's "degree" established superior and inferior ranks of people within society. Nature's rule distinguished the king or head of the state from his noblemen and citizens, the landlord from his serf, and the child from his father. Subordination of man to Nature's order gave him his degree and the rights and obligations linked with it. Man had to obey the civil law within the state which established order; this was based on the law of Nature which in turn was subordinated to God's eternal law by which God Himself had been working through the ages, generating life and order. Man's obedience to his civil law created harmony within the political body of his state, in the community in which he lived and in his family. Everything depended on man's God-given "disposition", i.e. the general constitution of his body, mind and character which influenced his every action.

→ **correspondence** [ˌkɒrɪ̵ˈspɒndəns] likeness between certain things
→ **macrocosm** [ˈmækraʊkɒzəm] the universe
→ **earthquake** [ɜːθkweɪk] a sudden shaking of the earth's surface, which may be violent enough to cause great damage
→ **eagle** [ˈiːgəl] Adler
→ **to recall** to remember
→ **cosmological** [ˌkɒzməʊˈlɒdʒɪkəl] having to do with the study of the origin and arrangement of the universe
→ **serf** [sɜːf] person (not quite a slave) forced to stay and work on his master's land, especially in a feudal system
→ **subordination** the act of placing o.s. in a position of lower rank; (here) obeying to s.b.

18 E. M. W. Tillyard, *The Elizabethan World Picture.* Harmondsworth: Penguin Books Ltd., 1963, repr., p. 34.

6.3.4. The optimistic and the pessimistic view of man

→ **liver** ['lɪvəʳ] Leber

Like all Creation around him man was made up of the four elements which he also found in the food he ate. These elements were converted by his liver, the centre of the lowest part of his body, into four "humours" (from the Latin *humidus:* 'moist'), basic liquids which were an important force of life within the human body. They could be influenced by a person's stars in his hour of birth, by periods of a man's life, by his food, or by the seasons of the year. Their mixture in the liver could change and thus alter his character and his outlook on life. Their four basic combinations determined a man's "complexion" (the colour of his face), his constitution and his character (i.e. the "disposition" of his mind and body). They were the following:

Element:	Quality in Nature and Man:	Humour:	Complexion:	Constitution:	Character:
Earth	cold and dry	melancholy	dark-coloured	lean	not cheerful, tending to think deeply about o.s., gloomy, etc.
Water	cold and moist	phlegmatic	pale	fat	inactive, lazy, slack and dull, etc.
Air	hot and moist	sanguine	ruddy, fair	fat	cheerful, courageous, in danger of being lustful or too optimistic, etc.
Fire	hot and dry	choleric	yellowish face	lean	tending to be angry, rash, proud, etc.

A word whose meaning came close to that of "complexion" was "temperament" (from the Latin *temperamentum:* 'proper mixture'), a term for the softening of one dominating humour through its mixture with other humours. By a set of complicated rules the Elizabethans explained the normal working of the humours in man's body. A disturbed balance of the humours led to illness in the mind and soul; e.g. melancholy. A man's temperament could be altered by a change in his dominating humour caused, for example, by too much heat in the liver. This could happen as a result of increased intensity of the passions which were seated in his heart, the organ governing the middle part of his body. The passions could be fired by imagination. If they took control of the topmost part of the body, they influenced a persons's will, using reason for their own purposes. Instead of helping man to distinguish between what was good or evil, reason then became a slave to passion. It encouraged man to live sinfully – which could easily lead to unhappiness in life and eternal damnation afterwards.

The struggle between reason on the one hand, and immoderate passion in his heroes' souls on the other, with subsequent breach of civil law and the law of Nature, is an important motif in both the tragedies and the histories which Shakespeare wrote. The resulting disorder not only affects the cosmos; it also disrupts the civil law within the state. Only by destroying the force responsible for disturbing the universal order can the existing natural and civil order be fully restored.

In spite of such pessimistic views of man and his world Shakespeare's age was also able to appreciate the beauty and order of Nature. The condition of the Earth after Adam's fall, the Earth's position at the lowest point of the universe, and man's limited ability to choose between reason and passion helped to explain the existence of two contradictory concepts – often existing side by side in Elizabethan people's minds – of the Earth and man's position in Nature. They contributed to the Renaissance conflict between an optimistic and a pessimistic view of man, society and the universe. On the one hand there was the Renaissance idea of man's dignity, his admired rank among Nature's creatures and his "definite place"[19] in a universe marked by degree and harmony. On the other hand, there existed the pessimistic medieval idea of a weak and sinful man who through Adam's original sin lost his right to everlasting life and his prominent position in the universe. Though he had been redeemed by God he was weak, self-centred and a servant to his passions. He was exposed to the varying influences of Nature, the stars and Fortune. Therefore it was doubtful whether man was to use what was left of his original willpower and reason. It was not certain whether man was able to keep order within the microcosm of his soul and to live as a useful member of a peaceful society.

This contradictory view of man was intensified by further doubts of man's high rank in creation and his world's central position in the universe. In his "Essais" (1580 and 1588) Montaigne expressed his doubts of the exact quality of man's theoretical knowledge and his traditional ethical standards, for man could easily be deceived by his senses and their constantly changing objects. Besides, man's opinions on what was good or evil were relative and varied from region to region.

When in 1543 Copernicus published his "De Revolutionibus Orbium Coelestium", he shattered the traditional astronomic conviction that the earth was the centre of the universe. According to his theory, the sun was the centre of the universe and the earth and the planets revolved around it. Long before this hypothesis was confirmed by Kepler in 1609 and Galilei in 1610 it was taken over by a small group of English astronomers. However, most of Shakespeare's contemporaries still believed in the geocentric cosmic system.

In 1602 traditional beliefs in natural and political order were further undermined when an English translation of Machiavelli's book "The Prince", written in 1513, was published in England. In it, Machiavelli had sought to give advice to an imaginary ruler who would free Italy from foreign occupation. He advised his "prince" to be a hard, even tyrannical ruler and not to care about moral standards if they stood in the way of his policies; he even advocated the use of evil practices if they were politi-

→ **ruddy** [ʌ] (of the face) pink and healthy-looking
→ **rash** [ræʃ] (of a person or his behaviour) foolishly bold, not thinking enough of the results
→ **to disrupt** [dɪsˈrʌpt] to bring into disorder
→ **contradictory** [ˌkɒntrəˈdɪktəri] serving to be opposite in nature or character to (another fact, action, statement, etc.)
→ **to redeem** [rɪˈdiːm] to buy or gain the freedom of, especially (in the Christian religion) the freedom from evil
→ **Fortune** [ˈfɔːtʃən] fate, chance, especially as an important influence on o's life; luck

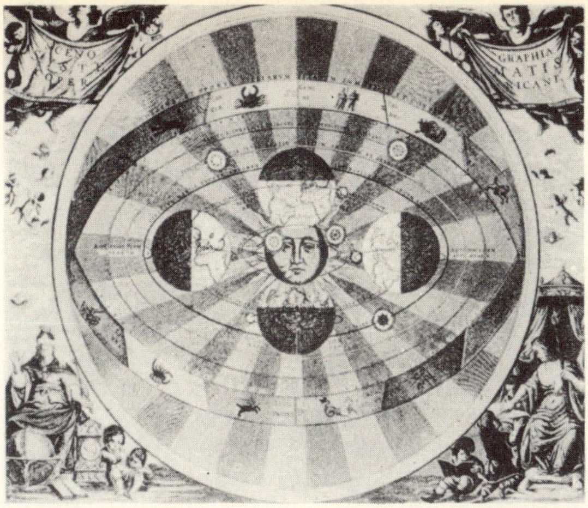

Copernicus' new view of the world, depicted in a contemporary illustration. The revolutionary new concept solved all difficulties of medieval astronomic calculations which always failed in agreeing with concrete observations. – A satisfied looking sun is residing in the centre sourrounded by the eliptic planets' orbits the most important of which is, of course, the earth: it is shown in four different positions according to day/night sides.

cally effective. In this way Machiavelli had separated politics and civil law from God's law and the law of Nature. He had created the picture of the evil politician, an idea which disturbed people as it destroyed their belief in good policy and honest government.

It is not surprising that Shakespeare's work, too, reflects the growing scepticism of his age about the order of the universe, the harmony of society and the ability of man to act rationally. The character of his RICHARD III, a clever outsider, may be identified with the coming New Man, the planning merchant or clever politician of Shakespeare's age. Richard manipulates human beings without any consideration of God's and Nature's laws and without caring about society, not respecting its values of honesty, order and cooperation.

In KING LEAR it is Edmund who shows the calculating spirit of a new age. He, too, refuses to accept the idea of Nature's origin from God and her ordering influence upon man and society who have to obey to what human reason discovers as natural. Edmund thinks that the stars have no influence on man who is superior to Nature and master of his own life. Edmund illustrates the fact that man regards Nature as a lifeless mechanism that follows indifferent rules of cause and effect. Man no longer uses his reason to obey Nature but to treat her as his object in order to master her, using her for his own needs. There are not only two different kinds of nature and two different sorts of reason in Shakespeare's age. Two separate concepts of society also exist. One of them is based on traditional medieval and Renaissance values of unity and subordination, represented, for example, by the person of an old monarch in KING LEAR. The other is the 'bourgeois' society of the dawning Capitalist era, whose members act as individuals, each for his own profit and influence. Its representative is the rational, clever politician who manipulates man for his own selfish purposes.

→ **bourgeois** ['bʊəʒwaː] of, related to, or typical of the middle class; (here also) persons more concerned with possessions and good manners than with ideas and feelings

→ **monarch** ['mɒnək]

19 Th. Spencer, *Shakespeare and the Nature of Man.* Lowell Lectures 1942. New York: Mac Millan Co., 1951, 2nd ed., reissue, p. VII.

6.3.5. Superstition

The Renaissance is regarded as the rebirth of Greek and Roman culture in all its forms, including scientific thought, and it was this scientific thought which, as time went on, developed new methods of exploring the world for the purpose of increasing trade with far-off lands. The Renaissance, however, must also be considered as an age of different Christian beliefs existing side by side with superstition. As a kind of religion without God, superstition was based on fear and ignorance. Its followers either imitated the worship of God by holding irrational ceremonies of worship which were beneath God's dignity, or they worshipped some real or invented powers instead of God. Those who practised superstition in both its Christian or pagan form tried to forecast or even control events in nature not by using the rational principle of cause and effect of modern technology but by using the art of magic. They turned to powers which they believed to exist outside the natural world for help in putting natural laws out of action.

With the Reformation English people, converted to Protestantism, were no longer able to ask Catholic priests to speak to the saints in Heaven on their behalf and for assistance in times of need. Those really in need of help went to the "good" or "bad" witches to ask their advice. In Shakespeare's age there were many old women who had paid rent for the use of farmhouses and land (they had been tenant farmers) but who had lost their income after being driven from their farms by landlords wanting to fence in their fields and the common land for more profitable sheep-raising. These impoverished women were often vagabonds or outsiders in those communities which were obliged to support them according to the Elizabethan Poor Laws in 1598 and 1601. These women could have tried to make a living by influencing the more fortunate people around them. Because of their unpleasant and perhaps dirty appearance they may have been associated with the devil or with supernatural powers. The "good" witches, wise old women, were able to help their neighbours, giving them advice on problems of life, or telling their futures. They may also have helped people by acting against the influence of "black magic" which was practised by the "evil" witches who intended to do harm in the name of Satan and with the assistance of their own servant demons. According to popular belief they were able to foretell the future, influence the weather, cause thunderstorms and winds, create illnesses in man and infect animals. They were also supposed to be able to vanish and appear whenever and wherever they wished, covering vast distances in no time. In spite of all this, the "evil" witches had no power to take away human life.

Besides the witches also magicians were believed to have power to ask good or evil spirits to help them. Queen Elizabeth herself is said to have asked a magician's help to protect her against a magic danger with the use of counter-magic. James I was strongly convinced that witchcraft existed. In 1597 he published a book entitled "Daemonologie" in which he described the activities of witches and asked his contemporaries to suppress witchcraft. In 1604, at the beginning of his reign, an Act laid down that relations with evil spirits were forbidden; it claimed the death pen-

After the disengagement from the Catholic Church all kinds of religious minorities tried to convince the people of their special variety in Christian faith. – The puritan tendency of one of them is expressed in this title page of a treatise against worldly pleasures on Sunday.

→ **beneath** not worthy of
→ **pagan** ['peɪgən] (of the ancient Greeks and Romans) connected with beliefs and practices of a person who believes in many gods
→ **to convert to** [–'–] to change o's religion
→ **magician** [mə'dʒɪʃən]
→ **impoverished** made poor

alty for acts of witchcraft which led to the injury or death of human beings. Similar Acts had been passed in 1542 and 1563.

Ghosts of dead people, especially those who were seeking revenge, were believed to rise from the graveyards after midnight and haunt the places of their former lives, carrying messages to those whom they wanted to influence. As "objective" ghosts in Shakespeare's plays they can be watched by several people at the same time. As "subjective" ghosts the apparitions of dead people are only perceived by their murderers by day or in dreams.

Like the usual ghosts the little playful fairies and the tiny, troublesome goblins appeared by night, playing bad or cruel tricks on human beings.

During the night the "sublunar" world of Shakespeare's dramas is also influenced by the rule of dark and evil forces which are thought to be personifications of bad human characteristics or activities. As soon as the Sun has left a certain region of the globe, Revenge, Murder, Rape, and other evil powers haunt the "nightside of the globe", fleeing light and committing deeds which frighten mankind. They have to leave the scene of their misdemeanour as soon as the dawning day, (i.e. the Sun's rays,) dispels their evil charm.

There are also personified good powers like Honour, Love and Fame which fill the regions of the sublunar world, using their helpful influence upon the characters in Shakespeare's plays. In MACBETH, for instance, there is a particularly large number of good, evil, or ambiguous mythological forces (e.g. Fortune, Chance, Death, Nature, Fate, etc.), moral powers and human attitudes (e.g. Valour, Justice, Villainies, Murder, Treason, etc.) and personified activities of the human mind (e.g. Pity, Dream, Sleep, etc.) which influence the characters' actions.

Astrology was a half-science. It was based on the belief that the constellations of Sun, Moon, Planets and Fixed Stars influenced both a man's character and his fate. The Middle Ages had developed the art of explaining positive or negative influences on life below the Moon's sphere from the position and constellation of the different stars. Each Planet had been given its special hour of influence. Therefore the success of many human activities such as medical, military or psychological operations depended on the calculation of the proper hour of a Planet's influence, or on the effects of a Constellation of Stars that offset another Planet's disturbing influence. This complicated medieval system, made simpler during the Renaissance, and preserved during the following centuries, still exists today.

Alchemy, another half-science, was concerned with finding a way of turning base metals into gold. People had noticed that iron changed into rust and so they believed that other substances such as lead could be changed into gold through finding what was called the philosopher's stone. Alchemists were also in search of an elixir which would provide a very long life. They also wanted to find a remedy for all diseases, a so-called "panacea" (from the Greek *panakés:* 'all-healing'). Alchemy was still practised in the 17th century when it led to the discovery of china and to the beginnings of medical chemistry.

→ **Daemonologie** [diːmə'nɒlədʒi] study of witchcraft
→ **graveyard** a piece of ground, often near a church, where people are buried
→ **apparition** [ˌæpə'rɪʃən] the spirit of a dead person moving in bodily form
→ **playful** gaily active, full of fun
→ **troublesome** causing trouble or anxiety; annoying
→ **goblin** a usually unkind or evil spirit which plays tricks on people
→ **to haunt** [ɔː] (of a spirit) to visit, appearing in a strange form
→ **rape** the act of having sex with a woman against her will
→ **misdemeanour** [ˌmɪsdɪ'miːnə^r] a crime that is less serious than, for example, stealing or murder
→ **to dispel** [–'–] to drive away
→ **ambiguous** [æm'bɪgjʊəs] able to be understood in more than one way, of unclear meaning
→ **villainies** ['vɪləniz] evil or wicked acts
→ **to offset** to balance
→ **alchemy** ['ælkəmi]
→ **lead** [led] Blei
→ **elixir** [ɪ'lɪksə^r] panacea [ˌpænə'sɪə]

A drawing, probably dating from the 16. Century. According to the pictures on the globe (and to the absence of a mathematician's instruments), it may portray an astrologer rather than an astronomer.

Part II: Close Reading of the Play

Act I, Scene 1

Exposition ★

Fair is foul, and foul is fair.

Phrases for discussing the scene

Audience and Effect

- **to be taken by surprise**
- the author's intention is to . . . (+ inf.)/the author intends to . . . (+ inf.)
- to genuinely ['dʒenjʊənli] believe in s.o. or s.th.
- there is something strange/mysterious [mɪ'stiəriəs] frightening, etc. about the scene

Setting

- **the scene takes place** . . . (where? when?)
- **before sunset**

Atmosphere

- **a violent thunderstorm is raging**/there is thunder and lightning
- a world of darkness/confusion/tumult ['tju:mʌlt]
- **the elements are at war**

Action

- a battle is being fought
- a rebellion is being suppressed
- the witches predict [prɪ'dɪkt] the future
- they announce a paradox ['pærədɒks]

Moral Order

- there is a reversal of good and evil
- **the scene introduces us to a world of political and moral confusion**
- 'fair' may mean both 'good' and 'beautiful'
- evil is accepted as good
- **opposites are the keynote of the scene**

Comprehension — **Unit 1**

1. State your first impressions after reading the scene (or hearing it on the tape, record, etc.).
2. Retell the scene in a few sentences.

3. Look at the map of Scotland and then describe the setting. ➧ Setting ➧ Stage Directions ●●
3.1. What three dramatic events are happening and developing parallel to one another here? ●●
3.2. To which spheres of human life and the universe do they belong? ●●
3.3 What do they have in common? ●●
4. How is the hero associated with these three dramatic events? Make use of your findings in (3.1.), (3.2.) and (3.3.). ➧ Protagonist ➧ Theme

Analysis

1. What is particularly striking about this scene? ●●
2. Which particular statements of the witches create an atmosphere of the supernatural, of horror, struggle, and evil? ➧ Atmosphere ●
3. Explain 'Fair is foul, and foul is fair' by giving the ➧ Literal Meaning and the ➧ Figurative Meaning of the two adjectives. ➧ Paradox ➧ Ambiguity ●
4. What effects of language are used in order to show the audience that this scene represents something extremely unusual and mysterious?

4.1. ➧ Assonance; ➧ Consonance Ⓖ
4.2. ➧ Anaphora; ➧ Rhyming Jingle Ⓖ
4.3. ➧ Rhyme; ➧ Iambus; ➧ Trochee. Ⓖ

Act I, Scene 2

Exposition ★

. . . Bellona's bridegroom, lapped in proof, . . .

Phrases for discussing the scene

Audience and Effect
- reported action (i.e. the use of messengers to report events) is a feature of the play
- **to arouse s.b.'s interest in . . .**

Information
- to learn about the battle and its outcome
- to bring news of . . .
- to paint a picture of . . .

Exhaustion
- to feel faint
- **to collapse** [kə'læps]

Fighting
- a furious battle is taking place
- the battle is not yet decided
- **to come face to face with**
- to take flight
- to begin a new assault [ə'sɔːlt]

Disloyalty and Punishment
- the battle is part of a revolt against . . .
- **the traitor is taken prisoner**
- to order s.o.'s execution

Bravery, Loyalty and Reward
- **to be presented as an almost mythological** [mɪθə'lɒdʒɪkl] **figure**

- to be superhumanly [ˌsuːpəˈhjuːmənli] brave and strong
- abstractions/abstract ['æbstrækt] concepts (e.g. vices and virtues) are used . . .
- to give s.o. a title/to bestow a title (up)on s.o./to invest s.o. with a title
- **the scene is dominated by . . .** — Atmosphere
- **there is ➧ Ambiguity** [ˌæmbɪˈgjuːɪti] in words such as . . .

Unit 2

Comprehension

1. Holinshed's CHRONICLES (1577) which provided the source material for Shakespeare's MACBETH mention 4 battlefields of 3 campaigns: a castle in Lochaber – Culross – Bertha Castle – Kingcorn. – Find the battlefields of this scene on the map of Scotland. ●●

1.1. Why couldn't the four battles have happend at the same time?

1.2. Why did Shakespeare combine them in one single event?

2. Give a short summary of the events shown and reported in this scene. ●

3. Paraphrase the text from line 7 to line 24. — ➧ Messenger's Report ●

4. In what way does the description of the battle remind us of Scene 1? — ➧ Leitmotif; ➧ Theme

Analysis

1. Analyse the simile contained in lines 25–28. ●●

1.1. Divide the simile into two parts. Which words are used to introduce each part?

1.2. What is expressed in each of these two parts? — ➧ Simile; ➧ Ground

2. Analyse the metaphor 'unseamed' in line 22. ●●

2.1. What are the associations of the word 'unseamed'?

2.2. What does the metaphor suggest about the character of Macbeth? — ➧ Metaphor; ➧ Figurative Meaning; ➧ Vehicle

Unit 3

Analysis

1. How is Act I, Scene 2 coloured by Revolt, Violence and Death? Find words indicating these three basic elements and the colour of blood which is associated with them again and again. — ➧ Atmosphere; ➧ Image ●●

2. How do these elements of the atmosphere, together with the thunderstorm and the witches in I,1 help to define the character of Macbeth? ●

3. What impression of Macbeth is given by the reports of the two eye-witnesses? ●●
   (Think also of the personified virtues and vices of the ➧ MORALITY PLAYS — ➧ Personification; ➧ Allegory

4. What is the function and the effect of the two separate messengers' reports? — ➧ Messenger's Report Ⓖ ○

5. What is suggested by King Duncan's words at the very end of the scene and by the fact that Macbeth is given Cawdor's title and lands? Ⓖ ○

6. What animal mataphors does this scene contain? What kind of associations do they have? Ⓖ ○

Text Production ●●

7. Study the following definition of the term 'Exposition'. Then try to explain the function of the first two scenes of MACBETH.

> In **Dramatic Structure** the *exposition* is the introductory material, which creates the tone, gives the **Setting,** introduces the characters, and supplies other facts necessary to an understanding of the play.[1]
>
> (Think of the length, the content and atmosphere of the first two scenes and consider what kind of picture of Macbeth is being built up.)

1 C. H. Holman, *A Handbook to Literature.* Indianapolis: The Odyssey Press, 1975, 3rd ed., p. 214.

Act I, Scene 3

Exposition ★
Rising Action

. . . and nothing is,
But what is not.

Phrases for discussing the scene

Drama

- **the author uses the dramatic device of the aside**
- in a soliloquy [sə'lɪləkwi] a character expresses the conflict in himself between emotion and reason
- there is a deliberate [dɪ'lɪbərət] ➧ Ambiguity in . . .

Psychological Reactions

- **to be amazed /astounded**
- **to be deep in thought**/to be carried away by one's thoughts
- to show self-control [ˌ––'–]
- to hope for the fulfilment of a prophecy ['prɒfəsi]

Thinking

- **it implies that . . .**
- to appreciate the trouble someone has taken
- to think in lifelike images

Language

- to use key words repeatedly
- **the ➧ Images are concerned with clothes, stormy weather, fear, etc.**
- ➧ Metaphors deepen the meaning of the central ideas of the play/ they form a colourful back-drop of associations and ideas/they make us associate . . . with . . .

Comprehension

Unit 4

Ⓖ ●●

1. Paraphrase the following lines:
   a) 51– 61
   b) 116–126
   c) 127–142
2. Give a summary of this scene of the play.
3. What Elizabethan beliefs about witches does this scene illustrate?

Analysis

1. State which parts of the scene belong to the external action of the play and which to the internal action. ●
2. Analyse the meaning and function of Macbeth's first speech (l. 38f.) ➧ Leitmotif ➧ Theme ●
3. Identify and explain the paradoxical elements in the witches' prophecies. ➧ Paradox Ⓖ ●
4. Explain the clothing metaphor and its function in ll. 108–109. Ⓖ ●
5. Discuss the meaning and dramatic function of the simile in ll. 144–146. ➧ Dramatic Function ➧ Simile Ⓖ ●

Analysis **Unit 5**

1. How do Macbeth's and Banquo's reactions to the witches' appearance and their prophecies differ? ●●
2. Study Macbeth's reactions to the fulfilment of the prophecy that he is to become Thane of Cawdor. ●●

2.1. Describe the development of his feelings in ll. 108–109 and 116–120. ➧ Monologue: Aside Ⓖ

2.2. Analyse Macbeth's soliloquy ll. 126–142: Ⓖ
   a) Underline those words which help you to divide the soliloquy up into thought units.
   b) Use your own words to summarize Macbeth's thoughts, feelings, reactions and conclusions. ➧ Monologue: Soliloquy

2.3. Underline some of the striking ➧ Figures of Speech. Explain their function in the text. Ⓖ

2.4. What do Macbeth's two shorter asides (ll. 143–144 and 146–147) tell us about his future strategy?

3. Summarize your findings in answer to (2.3.) and (2.4.). **Text Production**

Analysis **Unit 6** ☆

1. Analyse Banquo's reactions when he learns that the first prophecy has come true. ●●
2. At what point in the scene is it made clear to us that reality and unreality have begun to change places in Macbeth's mind?
3. Read the following definition of the ➧ Rising Action which begins after the Exposition. Then look at the questions and write down your findings in note form. Use these notes when giving your answers. ●

> The **Rising Action,** or **Complication,** is set in motion by the **Exciting Force** (In HAMLET the ghost's revelation to Hamlet of the murder) and continues through successive stages of **Conflict** between the **Hero** and the **Counterplayers** up to the **Climax** or turning point (in HAMLET the hesitating failure of the hero to kill Claudius at prayer).[2]

2 Holman, p. 173.

a) Where does the Rising Action begin in MACBETH? ➧ Rising Action ➧ Plot

b) What is the Exciting Force in this play? ➧ Exciting Force

c) What brief addition could be made to the above definition of ➧ Conflict to make it fit MACBETH better?

4. Comment on Banquo's remark about 'the instruments of darkness' in ll. 123–126. **Text Production** ➧ Theme ➧ Leitmotif

Act I, Scene 4

Rising Action ★

. . . Let not light see my black and deep desires;

Phrases for discussing the scene

Saying Things

- **to refer** [rɪ'fɜːʳ] **to s.th.**
- **to break off abruptly**

Making Preparations

- to make arrangements for the accommodation of someone
- to ride off in advance of the others
- the group disperses [dɪ'spɜːsəz] in order to . . .

Giving Praise

- to receive someone with praise and honour
- **to deserve praise**
- **there is no need for thanks**
- to do more than s.o. else can repay
- the title of . . . is conferred [kən'fɜːd] upon . . .

Trust

- to put one's trust in s.o./**to trust s.o.**
- **to judge by appearances**
- to read s.o.'s mind from his face

Moral Behaviour

- **to distinguish good from evil**
- to be confronted with an obstacle ['ɒbstəkəl]
- **to overcone a difficulty**
- to invoke evil forces
- to hide one's thoughts
- to commit a crime while shutting one's eyes to what one is doing

Growth

- to make a plant grow/to cultivate a plant
- **to use imagery** ['ɪmɪdʒəri] **of growth and gardening**

Comprehension

Unit 7

1. What happens in this scene? Summarize it in your own words.
2. Paraphrase the following lines: Ⓖ ●●
   a) lines 14–21
   b) lines 22–27
   c) lines 27–33

Analysis

1. In lines 11–14 King Duncan comments on the Thane of Cawdor's life and death. How do his words relate to the 'Fair is foul, and foul is fair'-theme and to the development of Macbeth's ambitious thoughts? ●● ➧ Dramatic Irony ➧ Dialogue
2. Duncan and Banquo use metaphors of growth, gardening, and farming in lines 28–29 and 32–33. ●●

2.1. What ideas about the natural order of things – about harmony in nature, in the state, and in man – are illustrated by this imagery?

2.2. How does this imagery fit in with the leitmotif of chaos and inverted order?

3. Consider Macbeth's reaction to the king's generous praise: ○

3.1. What commercial terms does he use in lines 22–27? ○

3.2. What do you think of the speech as a whole? (Remember that Macbeth is a feudal tenant [vassal] addressing his feudal lord [overlord].) ○

4. Comment on the progress in Macbeth's ambitious thoughts after King Duncan has appointed his son Malcolm his successor. ➧ Monologue: Aside
5. Is King Duncan a sentimental old man who is ruled more by his feelings than by reason and common sense? Give your own impressions of his character.

Act I, Scene 5

Rising Action

Hie thee hither,
That I may pour my
spirits in thine
ear . . .

Phrases for discussing the scene

Language

- **the letter is in prose**
- 'Must be provided for' is a euphemism ['juːfəmɪzəm] for 'must be murdered'

Thinking and Emotions

- **to be determined (to do s.th.)**
- **to be dominated by . . .**
- he shows his affection for her
- there is a deep intimacy ['ɪntəməsi] between . . .

Moral Attitudes and Values

- **to hesitate to commit a crime**
- to brood upon evil
- she calls upon evil spirits to take away her womanly qualities
- to place oneself in the hands of the devil
- **to be afraid that s.o. is too soft-hearted**
- **to act against o's conscience**
- to express inverted values
- **s.th. within a person revolts against an act**
- **to hide o.'s wicked thoughts by acting hypocritically** [ˌhɪpə'krɪtɪkəli]

Comprehension

Unit 8

➧ Prose
➧ Verse
➧ Rhythm

Ⓖ ●●

1. Paraphrase the following passages:
   a) lines 13–28
   b) lines 36–52
   c) lines 58–71
2. What important events does Macbeth not tell his wife about in his letter? Why is this?
3. What is shown by Macbeth's and his wife's manner of addressing one another? ●

Analysis

1. Analyse Lady Macbeth's first soliloquy (ll. 13–28). ●●
1.1. Divide her speech into its component parts.
1.2. Provide a heading for each section.
1.3. Name some of the striking ➧ Figures of Speech and explain their function in the soliloquy.
1.4. Describe Lady Macbeth's doubts and fears about her husband's character:
   a) First list those of Macbeth's character traits which are mentioned by his wife in lines 14–21.
   b) Then underline those words from the same passage which show you that she is judging the different elements of her husband's character on the basis of their probable degree of usefulness in the achievement of her ambition for him.
   c) Finally say what conclusions you draw about her moral standards and her character.

1.5. What do we learn about her ultimate aim, her immediate plans, and her allies?
2. Analyse Lady Macbeth's second soliloquy (ll. 36–52): ●●
2.1. Give a step-by-step account of her thoughts.
2.2. What is Lady Macbeth's purpose in making this speech? ➧ Invocation
2.3. Mark those words in the speech which express either good or evil powers, feelings, and actions and Lady Macbeth's attitude to them. Ⓖ ○
2.4. Then mark those words or passages in which Lady Macbeth speaks of unnatural or perverting influences in relationship to herself. Ⓖ ○
2.5. What conclusion can be drawn from your findings under (2.3.) and (2.4.) as to Lady Macbeth's character and moral nature? Ⓖ ○

Comprehension

Unit 9

1. The breathless messenger who has brought the news that the king is coming is compared in lines 36–37 to a hoarse raven. What does this metaphor convey?
2. In conversation with her husband Lady Macbeth speaks of 'providing for' the king and of the 'great business' that is to be carried out. ●

2.1. What does she mean?
2.2. What tactics is she using?
3. Why does Lady Macbeth only hint at her criminal intentions to Macbeth when in earlier passages in the same scene she has spoken openly of murder?

➧ Euphemism
➧ Dialogue

Analysis

1. When Lady Macbeth hears that the king is to be their guest her first reaction is to tell the messenger 'Thou'rt mad to say it' (l. 29). What does her exclamation show?
2. Compare Lady Macbeth's use of a milk metaphor when she talks about her husband (ll. 14–20) and her reference to her own milk when she calls upon the evil spirits (ll. 45–46):
2.1. Point out the similarities and differences between the two passages.
2.2. What attitude does she have to Macbeth's humanity?
3. The following scansion plan of Lady Macbeth's speech 'O never Shall sun . . .' (ll. 58–68) is provided in order to give some idea of the rhythmic structure underlying Shakespeare's verse. Study this scansion plan before answering the questions below:

1 x́ || x́ x →
2 x x́ x x́ x x́
3 x x́ | x x́ | x́ x x x́ | x x́ →
4 x x́ x x́ x || x x x́ x x́ | →
5 x́ x x x́ | x x́ x x́ x x́ |
6 x x́ | x x́ || x́ x x x́ x x x́ x
7 x x́ x x́ x x́ x || x́ x x́ x →
8 x́ x x x́ x x́ || x x́ x x́ →
9 x x́ x́ x́ x x x x́ x x́ ||
10 x x́ x x́ x x́ x x́ x x́ →
11 x x́ x x x́ x x́ x́ x́ x x

Symbols:
→ = run-on line
| = pause
|| = full stop, (semi) colon, exclamation mark

3.1. How many stressed syllables are there in each line? (Lines 1 and 2 should be counted as a single line.)
3.2. How many feet are there in each line?
3.3. What kind of verse foot is predominant?
3.4. Underline the deviations (i.e. irregularities) in lines 1–6.
3.5. Where and why is special emphasis given to particular words and ideas in the first six lines?
3.6. When and why are there pauses in lines 1–6?
3.7. What is the effect of the run-on lines?
3.8. Where and why is the tempo of the speech in lines 1–6 particularly fast or slow?
4. On the basis of the first few scenes of the play, discuss whether Lady Macbeth really seems to understand her husband's character.[3]

➧ Foot
➧ Enjambement
➧ Blank Verse

3 C. Brooks and R. B. Heilman, *Understanding Drama*. New York-Toronto: Holt Rinehart & Winston, 1948, repr., p. 668f.

Act I, Scene 6

Rising Action

. . . the heaven's breath
Smells wooingly here . . .

Phrases for discussing the scene

Ceremony of Reception

- the king and his attendants
- **to welcome a guest**
- to answer courteously ['kɜːtiəsli]
- to use elaborate [ɪ'læbəreɪt] language
- **to greet o.'s host**
- to display courtesy ['kɜːtəsi] and respect (to s.o.)
- to go to great lengths to try and please a special guest
- **to offer a service to s.o.**
- to bestow an honour (up)on s.o.
- **the castle is situated in pleasant surroundings**
- peace and harmony are suggested by images of love, growth, and religion
- a 'martlet' is a kind of bird, but it can sometimes mean a gullible ['gʌləbəl] person

Peaceful and Harmonious Atmosphere

Comprehension

Unit 10

1. Paraphrase lines 14–20. ●●
2. Summarize the events of this scene in your own words.
3. Suggest some reasons why King Duncan's and Lady Macbeth's language in this scene is so formal and elaborate.
4. Describe Duncan's opening words, in which he speaks of his impressions of Macbeth's castle. Pay special attention to the style of the speech and to the literary device used in the first phrase. ➧ Register ➧ Atmosphere ➧ Epithet: Transferred Epithet ●●
5. In lines 25–28 Lady Macbeth uses an image taken from the world of trade and money to describe the duties owed by a vassal and his wife to their overlord. What is this image, and what are the duties Lady Macbeth is referring to? (Make sure, first of all, that you know exactly what a 'vassal' is.) ●
6. Explain the simile in lines 23–24 and the metaphor that is linked with it. ●

Analysis

1. Explain the dramatic function of this scene. (Consider its atmosphere, and compare it to the atmosphere of the scenes that have gone before.) ●● ➧ Dramatic Function ➧ Dramatic
2. Compare the symbolic function of the raven in the last scene with that of the house martin here. ➧ Symbol ●

3. In Shakespeare's theatre, as there was no scenery, scene followed scene with scarcely any pause; and so the readiest, though not the only, way to vary the emotional pitch was to interpose a whole scene where tension was low between scenes where it was high.[4]

Does this observation fit Act I of MACBETH? Give reasons.

Text Production ●●

→ **the readiest** the most simple and convenient → **emotional pitch** the degree of feeling expressed, the intensity of impact on the audience → **to interpose** to put in (between two others) → **tension** excitement, horror, anticipation, etc., built up by the action of the play

Act I, Scene 7

Rising Action ★

'I dare do all that may become a man;/Who dares more, is none.'

Phrases for discussing the scene

- dark thoughts disturb s.o.'s peace of mind
- **to be torn between (one's) ambition and one's conscience**
- **to abandon** [ə'bændən] **o's plans**
- **to consider the arguments for and against s.th.**
- to commit a murder
- **to anticipate the horror of the deed**
- to be tortured by terrifying images of . . .
- to use honest means for dishonest ends
- **to have no conscience**
- **to be disloyal to . . .**
- to show o's contempt for s.o. or s.th.
- **to blame s.o. for s.th.**
- **to persuade s.o. to do s.th.**
- to urge s.o. to carry out a deed
- **to take risks**
- conditions are favourable for . . .
- to outline a plan
- **to give in to s.o.'s arguments**
- **the language refers to . . .**
- this passage contains images of . . .

Conscience

Emotions, Persuasion

Language

Comprehension

Unit 11 Ⓖ ●●

1. Paraphrase the following passages:
   a) lines 1–28
   b) lines 31–45
   c) lines 45–59
2. Retell the scene in a few sentences.
3. Who is wondering why Macbeth left the table before the end of supper?

4 A. C. Bradley, *Shakespearean Tragedy*. London: Macmillan, 1961, p 36f.

Analysis

1. Divide the scene into its component parts and explain why it may be described as a drama in miniature. ●
2. Analyse Macbeth's soliloquy (ll. 1–28): ●●

2.1. Begin by underlining the conjunctions, ordinal numbers and pronouns that introduce the separate ideas it contains.

2.2. Study the component parts of the soliloquy which you identified when you underlined the links in (2.1.) and provide headings for them. ●●

2.3. Study the sentence structure and the use of ➧ Figures of Speech: ○
   a) Make a list of the most striking syntactical and rhetorical devices;
   b) Explain their function within the text.

2.4. Illustrate the emotional and logical qualities of the soliloquy and its argumentative character. ○

2.5. Explain its dramatic function.
   a) What does it tell us about the development of Macbeth's mind?
   b) How does it relate to the rest of the scene?

3. What arguments and ideas are expressed in the clothing metaphors used by Macbeth and his wife in lines 32–35 and 35–38?
4. Give a short written comment on: **Text Production**
   I dare do all that may become a man;
   Who dares more, is none. (ll. 46–47)

Comprehension

Unit 12

1. Read lines 47–48. Are we to conclude that Macbeth and his wife had an earlier conversation about killing the king which does not appear in the play? Explain. ●

Analysis

1. Analyse Lady Macbeth's strategy when she tries to overcome her husband's scruples about killing the king (ll. 35–45 and 47–59): ●●

1.1. What arguments does she use?

1.2. Point out some of the rhetorical devices she uses to counteract the 'milk of human kindness' within him.

1.3. How effective are they?

1.4. What is it that shows that her appeal to the evil spirits to unsex her has been answered?

1.5. Summarize her strategy and evaluate it from the human angle.

2. Analyse Macbeth's doubts and fears at the end of this scene: ●●

2.1. What objections does he raise?

2.2. Try to decide how genuine they are by comparing them with the scruples expressed in his soliloquy.

2.3. What conclusions can we draw about Macbeth's attempts to harden his heart during the last few hours? ○
3. Analyse the final arguments Lady Macbeth uses to make her husband respond to her appeal and share her courage (ll. 60–72 and 78–80). ●●
3.1. Summarize the arguments.
3.2. What does the proposed murder plan tell you about Lady Macbeth's character?
4. Are Macbeth's scruples genuine? Discuss, in writing. **Text Production**
5. Compare Lady Macbeth's conclusions at I,5, 20–23 and her role in this scene. Are they consistent with one another? Give reasons for your answer.

Act II, Scene 1

Rising Action ★

'There's no such thing. It is the bloody business which informs Thus to mine eyes.'.

Hear it not, Duncan;

Phrases for discussing the scene

Atmosphere, Night and Suspicion

- it is past midnight
- the moon has (already) gone down
- the night tends to create bad thoughts
- **an atmosphere of sinister** [ˈsɪnɪstəʳ] **foreboding** [fɔːˈbəʊdɪŋ] **prevails**
- **to be troubled by premonitions** [ˌpreməˈnɪʃənz]
- to restrain evil thoughts
- **to be suspicious of s.o.**

- to be cautious — Ambiguity, Deception, Honesty
- to be a hypocrite ['hɪpəkrɪt]
- **to speak ambiguously** [æm'bɪgjuəsli]
- **to be unwilling to act dishonourably**
- **to keep o.'s. oath of allegiance** [ə'li:dʒəns]
- **to have a hallucination** [həˌlu:sɪ'neɪʃən] — Psychology, Vision and Decision
- the dagger is a hallucination brought forth by Macbeth's guilty conscience
- he tries to take hold of the dagger
- when darkness falls evil powers are at work
- to invoke/to call upon/to appeal to s.o. or s.th.
- his anguish is expressed in terrifying images

Comprehension

Unit 13

1. Carefully paraphrase Banquo's words at ll. 6–9 in simple language. — ➧ Monologue ●●
2. Summarize the events of the beginning of the scene (ll. 1–30) in your own words.
3. Point out the different ways in which Shakespeare establishes the time at the beginning of the scene.
4. How is suspense created in the first ten lines of the scene?
5. How does King Duncan show his gratitude for the Macbeths' hospitality? Ⓖ ●
6. What does Banquo mean when he tells Macbeth that the witches have shown him 'some truth' (ll. 20–21)? Ⓖ ●
7. Explain Macbeth's reaction and his secret thoughts (ll. 22–24). Ⓖ ●

Analysis

1. What elements help to establish the atmosphere of evil and approaching disaster at the beginning of II,1? (Remember Macbeth's and his wife's appeals to the stars (I,4,50) and to Night [I,5,48] — ➧ Image ●●
2. In Elizabethan and Jacobean English the word 'consent' had the following meanings: ●
   a) agreement, appointment, (i.e. agreement of time and place for meeting);
   b) opinion, advice;
   c) party or cause (i.e. political aims) or conspiracy (i.e. secret plan to do s.th. unlawful).

2.1. Which of these meanings fit the use of the word 'consent' in line 25? — ➧ Ambiguity

2.2. Explain Macbeth's motives and tactics in making this promise to Banquo.

3. Study the thoughts behind the exchange between Macbeth and Banquo on the subject of 'honour' (lines 25–29). Briefly answer the following two questions: — **Text Production**

3.1. What does Macbeth mean by the word 'honour' (l. 26)? (honour = (a) merit; (b) titles that reward it).
3.2. What does Banquo's reply mean?

Unit 14

Comprehension

1. Describe your impressions after reading Macbeth's monologue (ll. 33–64) or listening to it on tape or on record. ●
2. Paraphrase the monologue (ll. 33–64). ●●

Analysis

1. First study the contents of Macbeth's monologue: ●●
1.1. Read lines 33–49 and underline all the words concerned with seeing and touching. Explain what Macbeth sees or imagines he sees and wants to touch. Ⓖ
1.2. Look again at lines 33–49 and underline the words that indicate the mental events that occur in the course of the speech: (a) thoughts and feelings; (b) the beginnings of questions; (c) commands, and (d) statements (i.e. positive or negative expressions of facts or logical conclusions). Ⓖ
1.3. Read lines 33–64 and underline all personifications or implied personifications of objects, organs, human activities and supernatural powers. Show how Macbeth's imagination gives life to the tempting object and how he projects his individual situation upon nature, the dark hemisphere of the globe, and history. Ⓖ
2. Make use of your findings from (1.1.) to (1.3.) to work out the general structure of the monologue: ●●
2.1. Divide the speech into its main component parts. Give line numbers.
2.2. Provide a heading for each section. Write your headings down, leaving sufficient space below each heading for further notes.
2.3. Subdivide each section into smaller sense units. Use the more important puctuation marks in the text to help you. ○

Punctuation Marks:
? = question mark
: = colon
. = full stop
; = semicolon
- = dash

2.4. Choose some key words for each unit to sum it up and enter them under the headings you have already provided for the various sections of the speech. ○

Unit 15 ☆

Analysis

1. List some ➧ Figures of Speech (both rhetorical figures and tropes) you can find in Macbeth's monologue and explain their function.
2. Give an interpretation of the monologue: ●●
2.1. Making use of your findings from Unit 14, Analysis, 2.1. and 2.2.

➧ Dramatic Function

or 2.3. and 2.4., explain the dramatic function of Macbeth's monologue.

2.2. What evidence is there in the monologue that his vision is an evil one? Use your findings from Unit 14, Analysis, 1.3., 2.2. and Unit 15, Analysis, 2.1.

3. What is the symbolic significance of the bell Macbeth hears at the end of the scene? ➧ Symbol

4. Does Macbeth seem to be a sensitive, imaginative person? Give your opinion in a few sentences. **Text Production**

5. Explain, in a few sentences, the following quotation:
   Thou marshall'st me the way that I was going (II,1,42).

Act II, Scene 2

Rising Action

I am afraid to think what I have done: Look on't again I dare not.

Phrases for discussing the scene

Emotions, Feelings of Guilt

- a scene of horror
- **to be startled by . . .**
- to show traces of human feeling
- **to be in a state of nervous tension**
- to be mad with horror at the deed
- to regret the act bitterly
- his guilty conscience will prevent him from sleeping
- **he dare not look at his victim again**
- to be overcome by o's sense of guilt
- **to be made nervous by . . .**
- **to recover o.'s composure** [kəm'pəʊʒə^r] — Self-control and Criticism
- **to urge s.o. not to be faint-hearted**
- **to reproach s.o. for his loss of self-control** [ˌ– –'–]
- **to act as if one were brave**

Comprehension

Unit 16

1. Paraphrase the following lines: Ⓖ ●●
   a) ll. 1–15
   b) ll. 20–33
   c) ll. 34–39 and 56–68.
2. Retell the events of the scene.
3. Mark the speeches in which Lady Macbeth tries to influence her husband. ●

Analysis

1. Divide the scene into sense units. Justify your way of dividing it.
2. Analyse Lady Macbeth's and her husband's reactions to the sounds they hear and the things they see: ●●

2.1. What sights and sounds does she react to, and in what way?
2.2. What does Macbeth hear and see or remember hearing or seeing and what are his reactions?
2.3. What important difference is there between her anxieties and his fears?

➧ Interjection
➧ Exclamation

Comprehension

Unit 17

1. When and why does Lady Macbeth address Macbeth as 'My husband!'? ●
2. Contrast the criminal energies of Macbeth and Lady Macbeth as shown in this scene. (For example, which one of the two is able to look at the murdered king afterwards?)

Analysis

1. How does Lady Macbeth react to Macbeth's fears and scruples at what he sees and hears or imagines he has seen and heard? ●●
1.1. Quote some examples of her reproaches and analyse them.
1.2. Give quotations to show the facile (i.e. cheap) optimism of the arguments she uses to calm her husband.
1.3. When and why does she completely fail to understand her husband?
1.4. When does she seem to be impressed by what he sees, imagines, or thinks?
2. Is Lady Macbeth a woman with a limited ability to receive and react to impressions, or is she simply a woman who is capable of great self-control? Discuss.

Text Production

Act II, Scene 3

Rising Action ★

. . . 'T was a rough night.

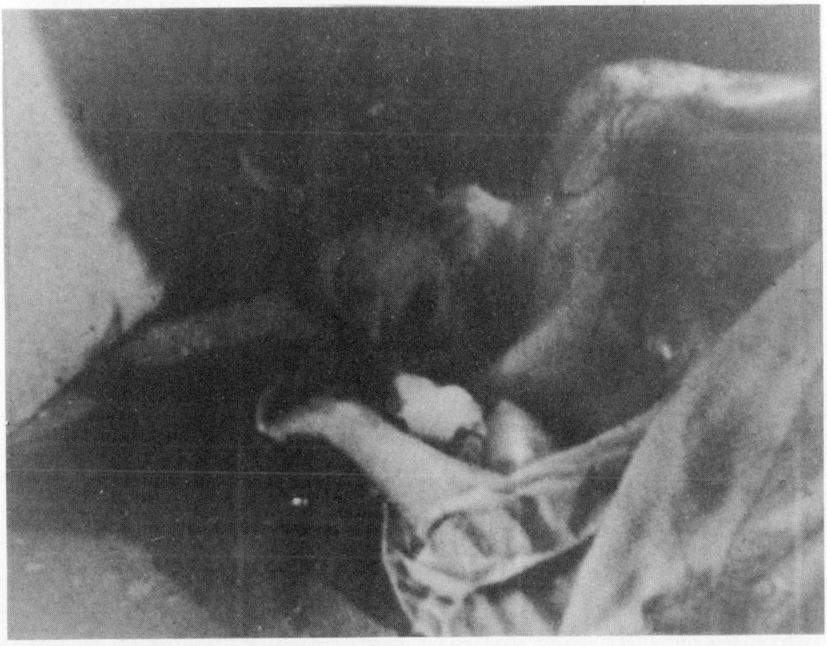

Phrases for discussing the scene

- **prose passages establish an ordinary level of communication**
- to return to verse — Verse and Prose
- blank verse is used to create a feeling of nobility or solemnity [sə'lemnəti] or to express powerful emotions
- the first part of the scene may be regarded as an interlude ['ɪntəlu:d] providing comic relief [rɪ'li:f] — Comic Relief
- **comic relief provides a brief pause in the tension built up during the preceding scenes**
- **to make jokes about dishonest people**
- **the drunken porter amuses himself by (+ ing-form)**
- s.o. pretends he is the porter of Hell Gate, a stock mystery play character
- Macbeth's castle has been turned into a place in Hell — Hell and Horror
- a moment of grimly serious farce [fɑ:s]
- **the stormy night reflects the disruption of the political order**
- revolt against the king is accompanied by disturbance in nature
- **to be horror-struck**/deeply shocked at the assassination of the king — Murder and Discovery
- **to be outraged** ['aʊtreɪdʒd]**/appalled** [ə'pɔ:ld] **at s.th.**
- **to act the role of the horrified host**
- **to faint**
- to give an unconvincing explanation of o.'s rash actions
- to express o.'s suspicions
- **an atmosphere of distrust** [dɪs'trʌst] **prevails**

Comprehension

Unit 18 ☆

1. Divide the scene into its component parts and then explain why you have divided it up as you have. Ⓖ ●
2. Describe the game the drunken porter is playing at the beginning of the scene. ➧ Interlude ➧ Foreshadowing ➧ Suspense Ⓖ ●
3. What do the three types of people who are admitted to hell have in common?
4. Describe and illustrate the various forms of humour in the porter's speech and in the dialogue between him and Macduff. ➧ Pun ➧ Comic Relief ➧ Sarcasm ➧ Allusion Ⓖ ●
5. Paraphrase the following lines: Ⓖ ●●
   a) 60– 69 and 69– 76
   b) 86– 92 and 105–115
   c) 124–130 and 136–144

Analysis

1. What elements link this scene with the earlier ones, providing continuity and contrast? ➧ Motif ●●

2. The porter scene provides comic relief. How does it also illustrate the idea that Macbeth's castle has turned into a kind of hell?

Text Production ●
➧ Morality Play
➧ Mystery Play
➧ Allusion

Unit 19

Comprehension

1. Make a list of the strange events in nature that take place during the night of the murder of King Duncan. ●

Analysis

1. Explain some of the images Macduff and Macbeth use in connection with:

1.1. the murder of King Duncan; Ⓖ
1.2. the victim himself; Ⓖ
1.3. the consequences of the murder. Ⓖ
1.4. What common ideas link these images?

2. Make use of your results from Unit 19, Comprehension: comment on the strange events in nature and their significance in relation to order within the state and in nature. ●●
3. Explain Banquo's answer to Lady Macbeth's exclamation 'Woe, alas! What! in our house?' (l. 83).
4. Have a closer look at Macbeth's reactions on ll. 86 ff. and ll. 105 ff.: ●●

4.1. What is the meaning of the first of these two speeches?
4.2 What does the second speech mean? (ll. 105 ff.)?
4.3. Analyse some of the striking ➧ Figures of Speech in the first passage and explain their function.

➧ Exclamation ○
➧ Alliteration
➧ Personification

4.4. Analyse some of the striking ➧ Figures of Speech in the second passage.

➧ Rhetorical Question ○
➧ Enumeration
➧ Metaphor ➧ Asyndeton
➧ Simile
➧ Personification
➧ Antithesis

4.5. Where does Macbeth seem to be expressing his true feelings and where does he sound dishonest?

5. What thoughts and events help to create a special atmosphere at the end of the scene? What atmosphere is this?
6. Explain in a few sentences why you think Lady Macbeth faints when the murder of the king is publicly revealed.

Text Production

Act II, Scene 4

Rising Action ☆

Thou seest, the heavens, as troubled with man's act,
Threatens his bloody stage

Phrases for discussing the scene

- **to relieve the tension**
- it has been the stormiest night within living memory
- the political and moral disorder is reflected in nature
- **day has turned into night**
- **everything has been turned upside down**
- the world is seen as a stage with human actors who are watched (and punished) by God
- **the scene focuses** ['fəʊkəsɪz] **upon the antagonist** [æn'tægənɪst] **Macduff**
- Macduff does not intend to be present at the coronation of Macbeth
- **to speak doubtfully about the future**

Disorder, Chaos

Theatre

Macduff, the Antagonist

Comprehension

Unit 20 ☆

1. Retell the scene in your own words.
2. Underline those words in which the events of the night are described as strange, unnatural and characterized by a state of rebellion. Ⓖ ●
3. Describe the extraordinary and terrible events of the night of Duncan's death. Ⓖ ●
4. What information does this scene give us about King Duncan, Macbeth, and the late king's sons? Ⓖ ●●

Analysis

1. Making use of your answers to Comprehension, 2. and 3., try to show how the characters on the stage express their sense of ●●

the relation between the murder of the king and the violent disorder in nature.

2. How does this scene make it clear that in spite of his growing success Macbeth will have to face a conflict which is no longer only a battle between his evil intentions and his conscience? ●●
3. Why do the old man's words at the end of the scene remind us of the leitmotif first heard at the end of the opening scene of the play?

Text Production ●

Act III, Scene 1

Rising Action ★

– To be thus is nothing,
But to be safely thus.

To be thus is nothing, But to be safely thus.

Phrases for discussing the scene

Hopes and Suspicions

- to ponder over s.o.'s success
- **the witches' prophecies have been fulfilled**
- Banquo recalls their other prophecy, that he will be the ancestor ['ænsəstəʳ] of a whole line of kings
- **to set o.'s hopes on s.th.**
- to suspect [sə'spekt] that s.o. has acted dishonourably
- to acquiesce [ˌækwi'es] in s.o.'s crime
- **to wait and see**

Fears and Aims

- to give a banquet ['bæŋkwɪ̵t]
- **to be afraid of no one but . . .**
- to realize that o.'s own guardian spirit is almost powerless against s.o. else's good spirit
- to display a growing sense of insecurity
- to give the impression of feverish ['fɪːvərɪʃ] activity
- to realize the futility of o.'s crime
- **to be faced with o.'s guilt**

- Macbeth wants to disprove the second part of the witches' prophecy
- **to challenge fate**
- **to have a secret interview with ...**
- to doubt s.o.'s manhood
- **to talk s.o. into believing s.th.**
- the murderers are persuaded that Banquo is their enemy
- a murderer is a desperate ['despərɪt] man
- they have friends in common whose trust Macbeth does not want to lose

Interviewing Murderers

Goes Fleance with you?

Comprehension

Unit 21

1. Put the following passages into modern English: Ⓖ ●●
   a) lines 1– 10 and 115–124;
   b) lines 47– 71;
   c) lines 90–107.
2. Give a summary of the scene in your own words.
3. Read ll. 1–10 again. Try to decide:

3.1. What Banquo thinks of Macbeth's reaction to the witches' first prophecies;

3.2. What Banquo thinks of the witches' prophecies about his own future, and what he intends to do about them.

4. Give a least two reasons why Macbeth wants to know when and how far Banquo is going and whether his son Fleance will accompany him. ●
5. Why does Macbeth fear Banquo and want to have him killed? ●●
6. What did Macbeth discuss with the two murderers during their first meeting? – Why has he sent for them a second time?
7. Why are the murderers willing to do whatever Macbeth tells them to do?

Analysis

1. Divide the scene up into its component parts. Briefly justify your way of dividing it up.
2. What developments in the internal and external action does this scene contain? ●●
3. Though Banquo must be regarded as an honest man, in some respects his behaviour is open to criticism. Explain. (Besides, looking at ll. 1–10 again, go back to Act II, Scene 3 and study his behaviour after the discovery of the murder of King Duncan.) ●
4. 'Propaganda' in our own day may be described as action taken by a government to influence public opinion by spreading true or false news, ideas or beliefs. ●●
   Does Macbeth, the tyrant who has just seized power in his country, use methods that may be regarded as propaganda?
5. Read Macbeth's soliloquy (ll. 47–71) and try to explain: **Text Production**
5.1. what Macbeth thinks of the fruits of his crime;
5.2. what he intends to do to prevent the fulfilment of the witches' prophecies about Banquo.

Analysis **Unit 22** ☆

1. Analyse Macbeth's technique in obtaining the cooperation of the old soldiers whom he hires to murder Banquo: ●●
1.1. Show how he uses the same argument which his wife successfully used in order to persuade him to commit his first crime. (cf. I,7, 49–51) ➧ Motif Ⓖ
1.2. Explain how Macbeth, like a modern dictator, makes use of hatred as an effective means of getting the co-operation of people who are dissatisfied with their low social status. Ⓖ
2. Macbeth may remind us of a modern ruler who has gained complete power over a country by force and is afraid of public opinion. Describe the steps Macbeth takes to deceive his people by masking his crimes, and explain his motives. (Look again at ll. 115–122, 123–125, 131–132) Ⓖ ●● ➧ Euphemism
3. Macbeth sometimes uses a comparatively harmless word for something evil which must not be explicitly mentioned. His euphemistic language makes us think of similar practices in modern totalitarian states. Give some examples of this technique from the present scene of the play. (cf. ll. 130–137) Ⓖ ●●
4. What differences are there between a tyrant like Macbeth and a modern dictator? (Think of Macbeth's relation to God, his conscience and his moral values. Compare this to the ideology of a modern dictator.) **Text Production** ●

Act III, Scene 2

Rising Action ★

*Nought's had, all's spent,
Where our desire is got without content . . .*

Phrases for discussing the scene

Psychological Reactions of Lady Macbeth

- **to feel frustrated**
- to realize the futility of o.'s efforts
- **to be full of doubts and misgivings**
- **to be weary** ['wɪəri]**/to lack sleep**
- to become passive
- to make half-hearted attempts to do s.th.
- a sense of guilt fills s.o.'s mind
- **what has been done cannot be put right**

Macbeth's Reactions

- **to feel insecure**
- to be full of evil designs
- **to be unsociable** [ʌn'səʊʃəbəl]
- **to be unable to repent**
- **to envy s.o.**
- his actions have all been to Banquo's advantage
- to be unwilling to disclose o.'s plans
- to detest flattery

Comprehension

Unit 23

Ⓖ ●

1. Paraphrase the following passages:
   a) lines 4–12 and 39–44;
   b) lines 13–26;
   c) lines 46–57.
2. Give a summary of this scene in your own words.

Analysis

1. Divide the scene into separate sections and justify your way of dividing it up. ●●
2. Describe Lady Macbeth's contradictory thoughts and feelings: ●●
2.1. when she is alone;
2.2. when she weakly attempts to encourage her restless and worried husband.
3. Examine the ambivalent ideas and statements contained in Macbeth's speeches to his wife and in his monologue at the end of the scene. ●●

Comprehension

Unit 24

1. What does Macbeth mean when he says 'O! full of scorpions is my mind, dear wife!' (l. 36)?
2. Why does Macbeth ask his wife to pay Banquo great respect and attention during the banquet when he knows that he will be dead by then?
3. Examine Macbeth's description of the night (ll. 51–57) and say what important ideas it expresses. ●●

Analysis

1. Compare Lady Macbeth's invocation of Night (I,5, 48–52) with Macbeth's (III,2, 47–51). Point out the similarities and the differences. Ⓖ

➧ Invocation

2. Explain why the following two lines from Lady Macbeth's soliloquy express the central idea of this scene: Ⓖ

   Nought's had, all's spent,
   Where our desire is got without content . . .

3. What is shown by the way Macbeth and his wife address each other, and by the fact that he does not tell her about his plan to have Banquo murdered? Ⓖ

Act III, Scene 3

The Turning-Point/ Crisis ☆

Fly, good Fleance,
fly, fly, fly!
Thou mayest revenge . . .

Phrases for discussing the scene

- **Fleance's escape marks the turning-point of the plot**
- **the scene takes place after sunset near Macbeth's castle**
- to ambush ['æmbʊʃ] s.o.
- to give a poetic description of the fading daylight
- **a third murderer joins the other two**
- to slay s.o.
- **to manage to escape/to succeed in escaping**
- **s.o.'s schemes** [ski:mz] **are foiled**
- Macbeth cannot control fate

Drama

Crime and Fate

Comprehension

Unit 25 ☆

1. Give a short summary of the scene.
2. Why do you think Macbeth has sent the third murderer? ●
3. Comment on the second murderer's statement: ●
   We have lost
   Best half of our affair. (l. 20)
4. What is your impression of the first murderer?

Analysis

1. What is dramatic about this scene? ➧ Dramatic Ⓖ ●
2. Why does Fleance's escape mark the turning-point in the fortunes of Macbeth? (Think of the witches' prophecies to Banquo.) Ⓖ ●●
3. What is the dramatic function of this short scene? ➧ Crisis ➧ Tragic Force Ⓖ ●●

4. Read the following passage about the 'critical point' in Shakespeare's tragedy and decide how the description fits MACBETH:

. . . In all the tragedies, though more clearly in some than in others, one side is distinctly felt to be on the whole advancing up to a certain point in the conflict, and then to be on the whole declining before the reaction of the other. There is therefore felt to be a critical point in the action, which proves also to be a turning point. It is critical sometimes in the sense that, until it is reached, the conflict is not, so to speak, clenched; one of the two sets of forces might subside, or a reconciliation might somehow be effected; while, as soon as it is reached, we feel this can no longer be. It is critical also because the advancing force has apparently asserted itself victoriously, gaining, if not all it could wish, still a very substantial advantage; whereas really it is on the point of turning downward towards its fall.[5]

→ **distinctly** [–'– –] clearly

→ **clenched** [klentʃt] in a position like that of two boxers who are holding each other firmly and tightly with their arms
→ **to subside** [–'–] to become quieter, weaker, or less active
→ **reconciliation** [ˌrekənsɪli'eɪʃən] renewed peace or friendship
→ **to assert o.s.** [ə'sɜːt] to act in a way that shows o.'s power or authority
→ **to be on the point of doing s.th.** to be just about to do s.th.

5 Bradley, p. 38f.

Act III, Scene 4

The Counterblow ★

You have displaced the mirth, broke the good meeting
With a most admired disorder.

Avaunt! and quit my sight!

Phrases for discussing the scene

A Banquet and its Sudden Interruption

- **the guests are welcomed in a polite and friendly manner**
- to take o.'s place according to o.'s rank
- to urge s.o. to do s.th.

- **to perform o.'s duties as a host** [həʊst]
- **to propose a toast (to s.o.)**
- **to express regret for s.o.'s absence**
- the atmosphere of friendliness and harmony is destroyed
- to dismiss o.'s guests before the meal is over
- to ignore the order of precedence ['presɪdəns]
- **to have a fit of terror** — Psychological Reactions:
- to rid o.s. of a hallucination [həˌluːsɪ'neɪʃən] — a) Macbeth
- **to be dazed** [deɪzd]
- to increase people's suspicion
- **to show presence of mind** — b) Lady Macbeth
- **to come to s.o.'s aid**
- **to save s.o. from detection**

Unit 26

Comprehension

1. Paraphrase the following passages: Ⓖ ●●
   a) lines 1– 6, 12–19, 128–144;
   b) lines 40–43, 50–52, 60–68, 128–144;
   c) lines 85–91, 93–110, 110–116.

Analysis

1. Divide the scene into sense units. Explain when and how the main action is interrupted, accompanied, or followed by other dramatic elements. ●●
2. Try to integrate the different sense units of this scene into two different strands of action: events connected with those of the previous scene, and events making up the main action. Find a title for each of the two sequences of action. ●●
3. Work out the symbolic function of this scene. Think of the elaborate state ceremony of the banquet and the moral order which disrupts it. ➔ Symbol ➔ Theme ●●

Unit 27

Comprehension

1. Where in his exchanges with the murderers does Macbeth use ambiguous words to soften the fact of his crime? ●● ➔ Euphemism ➔ Ambiguity
2. Which of Macbeth's phrases or actions serve as cues (i.e. signals) for the entrance of Banquo's ghost? ➔ Dramatic Irony
3. How does Shakespeare indicate to us that Banquo's ghost is seen only by Macbeth?
4. When Macbeth is frightened almost to death by the appearance of Banquo's ghost Lady Macbeth scolds him several times, casting doubt upon his manhood. How does he react? Ⓖ ●
5. At what point does Lady Macbeth show great presence of mind? Ⓖ ●
6. What does Macbeth decide to do when he is alone with his wife after the banquet has broken up in disorder? Ⓖ ● ➔ Monologue: Soliloquy

Analysis

1. Analyse Macbeth's feelings and behaviour in the various phases of the scene, and identify the four different roles he plays during and after the banquet. ●●
2. How does Macbeth show that – like a modern dictator – he employs a kind of Secret Police to spy on the prominent people of the country? ●●
3. What do Macbeth's words at lines 135–140, and at lines 142–144, tell us about his moral development? ●●
4. Read the following passage and decide whether it applies to this play. Then comment briefly: ●●

The crisis in which the ascending force reaches its zenith is followed quickly, or even without the slightest pause, by a reverse or counter-blow not less emphatic and in some cases even more exciting. And the effect is to make us feel a sudden and tragic change in the direction of the movement, which, after ascending more or less gradually, now turns sharply downward.[6]

Text Production
➧ Climax
➧ Crisis
➧ Falling Action

→ **zenith** ['zenɪθ] the highest point, e.g., of s.o.'s fortunes
→ **reverse** defeat or change for the worse
→ **emphatic** [-'--] forceful, especially in its effect on the audience

6 Bradley, p. 44.

Act III, Scene 5

Falling Action ☆

And you all know, security
Is mortals' chiefest enemy.

Phrases for discussing the scene

Witches

- **to do s.th. without asking s.o.'s advice**
- **to express o.'s disapproval**
- **to make up for the harm one has done**
- to deceive s.o. with ambiguous prophecies
- to be given a fatal ['feɪtl] sense of security

Comprehension

Unit 28 ☆

1. What does Hecate complain to the witches about?
2. How are the witches to make up for their past mistakes?
3. Describe how Macbeth is to be led to his destruction.

Analysis

1. What makes the critics say that this scene is not by Shakespeare but was inserted later by another dramatist? (Think of the implicit concept of man in Shakespeare's tragedies, according to which a person's character is his destiny. How does this fit in with the present scene and its implications?) ●

Act III, Scene 6

Falling Action

. . . that a swift blessing
May soon return to this
our suffering country
Under a hand accursed!

Phrases for discussing the scene

Talk

- to speak ironically [ɪ'rɒnɪkəli]
- **to change the subject**

Oppression

- the country is oppressed by tyranny ['tɪrəni]
- **to fear for o.'s life**
- to be no longer able to eat/sleep in peace

Opposition

- **to flee (to another country)**
- **to overthrow a ruler/despot** ['despɒt] **, etc.**
- **the opposition has begun to gather**
- to send an army to liberate a country
- **to encourage s.o. to do s.th.**

Comprehension

Unit 29

1. Paraphrase lines 1–20. ●●
2. Summarize the 'things' that (according to Lenox) 'have been strangely borne' recently. ●
3. What other facts indicate that Macbeth's tyranny is oppressing the country with terror and murder? ●●
4. What signs are there of growing opposition to Macbeth's tyranny? ●

Analysis

1. Have a closer look at Lenox' first speech: ●●

1.1. List some of the rhetorical devices he uses in lines 1–20.

1.2. Decide what their function is within the speech.

➧ Rhetorical Figures
➧ Interjection
➧ Rhetorical Question
➧ Swear Word
➧ Intensifying Adverb
➧ Attitudinal Adverb

1.3. Describe the ➧ Tone of Lenox' statements.

2. What is the advantage of using irony in a country under tyrannical rule? ●●
3. What supernatural powers are expected to help in the fight against Macbeth's tyranny? ●

➧ Theme

Act IV, Scene 1

Falling Action ★

Infected be the air whereon they ride: And damned all those that trust them!

By the pricking of my thumbs, something wicked this way comes.

Phrases for discussing the scene

The Witches' Activities

- **to perform a magic ritual** ['rɪtʃʊəl]
- to bring forth an apparition
- **to deceive s.o.** (by doing s.th.)
- to encourage s.o. to continue his course
- **to dissuade** [dɪ'sweɪd] **s.o. from doing s.th.**
- **the apparitions anticipate** [æn'tɪsɪpeɪt] **future events**
- the witches vanish

Macbeth's Behaviour

- **to insist upon s.th./that . . .**
- he does not care if the world is destroyed in the process
- to silence the voice of conscience within o.s.
- Macbeth has given himself up to the agents of evil
- **to be filled with false confidence**
- **to be troubled by s.th.**

Comprehension

Unit 30

1. Summarize the scene in your own words.
2. Put the following passages into modern English: ●●
   a) lines 94–103
   b) lines 144–152
3. Analyse Macbeth's long speech to the witches (ll. 50–61):
3.1. What does he want to do?
3.2. Is there anything that strikes you from the formal point of view about this speech?
3.3. What does this passage tell us about Macbeth's state of mind?
4. What are the first three apparitions and what do they signify? ●●
5. What is the meaning of the final series of apparitions? ●●

Analysis

1. How does Macbeth show that his moral character has deteriorated? ●●
2. What is the dramatic function of Macbeth's curse at lines 133–134?
3. Discuss the points raised in this passage: ●

Why does Macbeth return to the witches? Does he really expect them to recall their prophecy concerning Banquo's children? May one state his dilemma in this way: if the witches really know the future, then the future is fixed and it cannot be altered by having the witches unsay what they have prophesied concerning Banquo's children; if the witches do not know the future, then a comforting prophecy from them is of no value anyway? Or, may one put the matter thus: Macbeth wants to eat his cake and have it: he wants the witches to tell the truth with regard to his fortunes – but falsehoods with regard to Banquo's?[7]

→ **to recall** to take back, to say that what one has said before is untrue
→ **to unsay** [–'–] to recall (see above)

→ **comforting** [ˈkʌmfətɪŋ] positive, pleasing

→ **to eat o.'s cake and have it** to have the advantages of s.th. without the disadvantages that go with it
→ **with regard to** about, concerning
→ **his fortunes** the good or bad things that will happen to him

7 Brooks, Heilman, p. 670.

Act IV, Scene 2

Falling Action ★

. . . when our actions do not,
Our fears do make us traitors.

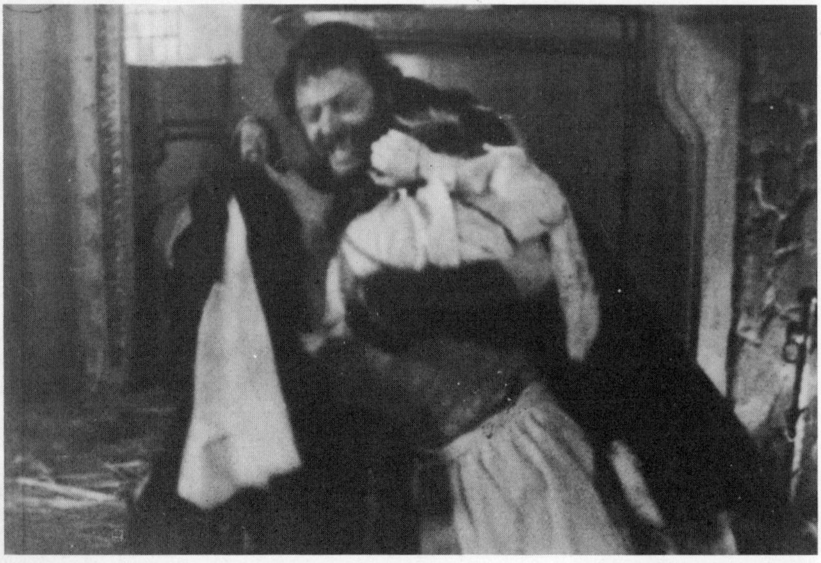

"Murder!"

Phrases for discussing the scene

Dramatic Function of the Scene

- **the scene dramatizes** ['dræmətaɪzɪz] **the horror of Macbeth's tyranny**
- **to hold s.o. responsible for s.th.**
- to create distrust [dɪs'trʌst] between (people)
- **to have innocent people killed**

Lady Macduff's Behaviour

- Lady Macduff does not know what to think of her husband's flight
- to seem like an admission of guilt
- **to be unaware** [ˌʌnə'weəʳ] **of the real motives**
- a dialogue which is full of pathos ['peɪθɒs]

Macduff's Son and his Fate

- **to be precocious** [prɪ'kəʊʃəs]
- to know the (wicked) ways of the world
- **to stand up for s.th. or s.o.**
- to stab s.o. to death
- **to pursue** [pə'sjuː] **s.o. on stage/off stage**

Comprehension

Unit 31

1. Paraphrase the following passages: ●●
   a) lines 12–14 and 18–22;
   b) lines 70–76.
2. What complaints does Lady Macduff make against her husband? ●●
3. Give a summary of Lady Macduff's amusing dialogue with her son.

Analysis

1. Divide the scene into sense units und justify your way of dividing it up. ●
2. Explain how this scene serves to illustrate the horror and the growing evil resulting from Macbeth's tyranny. ●●
3. Give examples from the text to illustrate the fact that several political attitudes or reactions to a tyrannical government are possible. ●●
4. Discuss: Is the mother and son's defiance of the murderers symbolic or not? Give reasons for your opinion. ●●

➧ Symbol

Act IV, Scene 3, 1st part

ll. 1.-138

Falling Action

Be comforted: Let's make us medicines of our great revenge . . .

*That which you are, my thoughts cannot transpose:
Angels are bright still, though the brightest fell . . .*

Phrases for discussing the scene

Malcolm's Strategy and Arguments

- to be wary ['weəri] of s.o. or s.th.
- to accuse o.s. of having vices/being wicked, etc.
- **to test s.o.** (or s.o.'s character, patriotism, etc.)
- **to express doubt**/to have o.'s doubts about s.th.
- **to leave s.o. at the mercy of a tyrant,** etc.
- to declare that one has no virtues
- **to be convinced of a person's integrity**
- to promise s.o. one's support

Macduff's Reactions

- to insist upon s.th./insist that . . .
- **to be upset about/hurt by s.o.'s suspicions**
- to play down the importance of s.th.
- **to lose patience with s.o.**

Function of the Scene

- **it provides a kind of choric** ['kɒrɪk] **comment** ['kɒment] **(on s.th.)**

Comprehension

Unit 32

Ⓖ ●●

1. Paraphrase the following passages:
   a) lines 8– 17, 18–24, 114–125;
   b) lines 25– 31, 43–54, 114–125;
   c) lines 91–100, 102–114, 114–125.

Analysis

●●

1. Malcolm first tests Macduff's loyalty by expressing a certain attitude towards him (lines 8–44):

1.1. What attitude does he express?

1.2. What arguments does he use to express his opinion of him?
2. What new test of Macduff's integrity does he then try (ll. 44 ff.)? ●●
2.1. What vices does Malcolm attribute to himself?
2.2. Which of the three vices is the worst, in Macduff's eyes? Explain why. ○
3. Can you name some of the far-reaching effects of Macbeth's tyranny demonstrated in this scene? ●
4. Malcolm's false confession is like a mirror reflecting the wickedness of Macbeth, and the speech in which he withdraws it depicts the virtues of the ideal king. What are these virtues that a good king should have? Try to divide your list into three: characteristically Roman, Germanic, and Christian virtues. ○

Act IV, Scene 3, 2nd part

ll. 139-240

Falling Action ★

Macbeth is ripe for shaking, and the powers above Put on their instruments.

Bring thou this fiend of Scotland and myself; within my sword's length set him; if he 'scape, heaven forgive him too!

Phrases for discussing the scene

The Living Image of a King of God's Grace

- Edward, King of England, is presented as a priest-king of God's Grace
- **he serves as a foil to Macbeth**
- **to cure/heal a person** (to cure a disease, to heal a wound)
- **to inherit s.th. from s.o.**/s.th. is handed down from one person to another
- to have the gift of prophecy ['prɒfəsi]

Macbeth's Tyranny in Scotland

- things are very bad in Scotland
- the country is ruled by fear

- **to rise in rebellion/rebel** [–'–] against s.o.
- **to join forces (with s.o.)**
- to inform s.o. of s.th./**to break the news of s.th. to s.o.**
- **to be struck (stricken) with grief**/to be grief-stricken
- **to avenge s.o.'s death**
- to revenge o.s. (up)on s.o. for s.th./to take revenge on s.o. for s.th.

Macduff's Behaviour

Comprehension

Unit 33

1. What do we learn about the situation of the Scottish people under Macbeth's tyranny? ●
2. What do we learn about the growing resistance to Macbeth's tyranny in Scotland and abroad? ●●

Analysis

1. Show how the description of the English priest-king serves as a foil to Macbeth's tyranny: ●

1.1. Make a list setting out and explaining the principal gifts of this king. Then add a statement of the ways in which Macbeth differs from Edward.

1.2. Compare the effect of Edward's rule on the English people with the effect of Macbeth's on the Scots. (Think of each king's relation to God or the Devil [1.1.], and of the type of ruler each represents [1.2.].)

2. What Christian ideas are used to characterize the opposing parties and their allies? ●

Act V, Scene 1

Catastrophe ★

Unnatural deeds
Do breed unnatural
troubles . . .

Out, damned spot! out, I say!

Phrases for discussing the scene

Lady Macbeth's Breakdown

- **to be terrified of the dark**
- to place a candle at s.o.'s bedside
- **s.o.'s mind is disturbed**
- **to go mad**
- to walk in o.'s sleep
- **to act out past events**
- **to call up images in o.'s mind**
- to suppress o.'s conscience
- to talk disconnectedly [ˌdɪskə'nektɪdli] (about s.th.)

Consideration of her Illness

- **to witness s.th.**/to be a witness to s.th.
- to be bewildered by s.th.
- **to look after a sick person**
- to confess o.'s sins to a priest
- **to commit suicide** ['suːɪsaɪd]

Unit 34

Comprehension

1. Retell the scene in your own words.
2. What is remarkable about Lady Macbeth's sleep-walking? ●●
3. Why does the lady-in-waiting refuse to tell the doctor what she has heard her sleep-walking mistress say? ●
4. Give examples of how Lady Macbeth's mind acts like a magic lantern which projects disconnected pictures drawn from her guilty memories before her consciousness, to the accompaniment of imagined words and sounds. ●

Analysis

1. Lady Macbeth's state of mental disturbance gives us a glimpse of a soul tortured by guilty memories. Describe how. ●●
2. Comment upon the doctor's diagnosis (lines 59–62).

Act V, Scenes 2–3

Catastrophe

... Hang those that talk of fear.

The English power is near, led on by Malcolm ...

Phrases for discussing the scenes

The Military Situation

- to join forces with s.o. against s.o. else
- **to meet up with s.o.**
- to fortify a castle
- **to give o.'s life/o.'s blood for a cause**

Macbeth's Reactions

- **to be irritable** ['ɪrɪtəbəl]
- **to be sick at heart**
- to give s.o. false hopes/false confidence

Comprehension

Unit 35

1. What do we learn about the military situation in Scenes 2 and 3? ●●
2. What significant difference in fighting spirit is there between the Scottish patriots and Macbeth's troops? ●

Analysis

1. In Scene 2 of this act rumours are quoted to the effect that Macbeth is 'mad' or at least showing 'valiant fury' (ll. 13–14). How does Macbeth confirm them by his behaviour in the following scene? ●●
2. Explain how the two clothing metaphors at V, 2, 15–16 and 20–22 help to illustrate the decline of Macbeth's fortunes. ●●
3. At V, 2, 29–31 Lenox uses a gardening metaphor.

3.1. What ideas does this express?

3.2. What associations link the passage to earlier uses of the gardening metaphor by Duncan and Banquo at I, 4, 28–29 and I, 4, 32–33?

Unit 36

Comprehension

1. How does Macbeth show that he still believes in the truth of the witches' prophecies? ●
2. When asked what he thinks of Lady Macbeth's mental derangement the doctor gives an answer which corresponds to the findings of modern medical science (V. 3, 45–46). Try to explain.

Analysis

1. Analyse the thoughts and wishes that Macbeth expresses to the doctor at V, 3, 39–45:
1.1. What does he ask the doctor to do?
1.2. What realization about his wife's illness does he express?
1.3. Analyse the most striking ➧ Figures of Speech (rhetorical devices and tropes) of this passage. ○
1.4. Discuss the effect of these figures of speech on the listener. ○
2. At V, 2, 27–29 a Scottish patriot speaks of healing his country's 'sickly' state. In his conversation with the doctor Macbeth himself speaks of his country's 'disease' (V, 3, 50–56). Comment on the similarities and differences between the two passages.
3. Why is Macbeth 'sick at heart' (V, 3, 19)? (Think of the knowledge he has gained about his own life and about life and human values in general. Make a step-by-step analysis of the text.) ●●
4. Explain why Macbeth reminds the modern reader of a 20th-century dictator: ●●
4.1. How does he treat the people around him? Ⓖ
4.2. Describe the feelings and attitudes of the people around him. Ⓖ
4.3. Explain how he uses terror in order to stabilize his military position. Ⓖ

Text Production

5. Read the following passage and relate at least three of the writer's principal statements to MACBETH.

. . . A study of the imagery in Shakespeare's tragedies helps us to appreciate them as an organization in which all the parts are interrelated and mutually attuned. Each tragedy has its own unmistakable individual nature, its own colour; it has its own landscape, its own atmosphere, its own diction. All details are closely connected, as in a finely meshed web; they are mutually dependent and point ahead or hark back. It is amazing to observe what part the imagery plays in helping to make the dramatic texture coherent as well as intricate. The same motif which was touched upon in the first act through the imagery, is taken up again in the second; it undergoes a fuller execution and expansion perhaps in the third or fourth. As Professor Spurgeon has demonstrated, these 'leitmotifs' of the imagery run through the play like a brightly coloured thred. Of 'Macbeth' it has been noted with acumen that Shakespeare substitutes the unity of atmosphere for the dramatic unities of time and action. [Max Deutschbein, *Macbeth als Drama des Barocks,* Leipzig 1936] This is true of many of the Shakespearean tragedies. This unity of atmosphere and

→ **to appreciate** to understand and value
→ **mutually attuned** [ə'tju:nd] in harmony with one another
→ **diction** choice of words and phrases (in poetry)
→ **a finely meshed web** a net closely woven out of thin threads (e.g. by the spider to catch flies)
→ **to hark back** to point backwards (i.e. to be related to earlier passages in the play)
→ **texture** an author's handling of the mass of details which a literary structure is made of
→ **intricate** ['ɪntrɪkət] complicated
→ **Spurgeon,** [ɜ:] Caroline (1869–1942): an English scholar

mood is no less a 'dramatic unity' than the classical dramatic unities. And the imagery of a tragedy plays an important part, not only in creating a dramatic unity of atmosphere, but also in binding the separate elements of the play together into a real organic structure.[8]

who wrote a book on *Shakespeare's Imagery* (1935) which threw new light on the poet and his works
→ **acumen** ['ækjʊmən] great intelligence

Act V, Scenes 4–5

Catastrophe ★

The queen, my lord, is dead.

I 'gin to be aweary of the sun,
And wish th' estate o' th' world were now undone.

Phrases for discussing the scenes

Macbeth's Crumbling Defences

- **to besiege** [bɪ'siːdʒ]**/lay siege to a castle, etc.**
- **to close in on s.o. (from all sides)**
- to make a strategic [strə'tiːdʒɪk] blunder
- to hold out against a siege
- **to fight to the end**/to the last man

Macbeth's Reaction to his Wife's Death

- to be preoccupied [priː'ɒkjʊpaɪd] with s.th.
- **to be overcome by (nihilism** ['naɪɪ̵lɪzəm], **despair, etc.)**
- life is/aims are futile ['fjuːtaɪl]/pointless/worthless
- **to enact** [ɪ'nækt] **a play**
- **to be weary** ['wɪəri] of life
- to be determined to die fighting

8 W. H. Clemen, *The Development of Shakespeare's Imagery.* London: Methuen, 1966, repr., p. 104f.

Unit 37

Comprehension

1. Paraphrase the following passages: V, 5, 9–15; V, 5, 17–28.
2. How is the collapse of the tyrant's defence forces shown in these two short scenes?
3. Explain the strategic blunder (i.e. military error) Macbeth makes when he learns about the moving wood. (Think of his boast about the strength of his castle [V, 5, 1–6], and of his fatal order [V, 5, 46].)

and now a wood comes toward Dunsinane.

Analysis

1. When Macbeth hears the women scream he uses a food metaphor:

1.1. What do his words reveal about the development of his character and about his present state of mind?

1.2. What figures of speech make the passage impressive? Explain their function.

2. Examine Macbeth's reaction when he learns of his wife's death:

2.1. Divide Macbeth's speech up according to the different stages of his thought.

2.2. Summarize each section by quoting a few key words.

2.3. What has happened to his love for his wife?

2.4. What images does he use to describe human life?

2.5. Analyse these images and say what they tell us about his attitudes.

3. Do a step-by-step analysis of Macbeth's thoughts when he is told that Birnam Wood is moving (V, 5, 35–52):

3.1. Give an outline of his speech and analyse its structure.

3.2. Why does he react so violently?

3.3. Explain why he does not completely lose the sympathy of the audience.

4. Read the following two quotations from a book on Hitler's Germany by an English historian. Draw parallels between the two tyrants' statements and behaviour, without losing sight of the personal and historical differences.

a) . . . Hitler spoke now as he had spoken in conversation with Rauschning before he was in power: "We may be destroyed, but if we are, we shall drag a world with us – a world in flames. . . ."[9]

b) . . . When in the middle of January 1945 he moved into residence in the Reich Chancellery, with its substantial underground bunkers, he was a broken man. Guderian and others have described his physical condition: "It was no longer simply his left hand but the whole left side of his body that trembled. . , . He now walked awkwardly, he stooped more than ever, and his gestures were both jerky and slow." At the same time he was subject to terrifying fits of rage. "His fists raised, his cheeks flushed with rage, his whole body trembling, the man stood there in front of me", as Guderian described one such occasion, "beside himself with fury and having lost all self-control. After each outburst of rage Hitler would stride up and down the carpet edge, then suddenly stop immediately before me and hurl his next accusation in my face. He was almost screaming, his eyes seemed about to pop out of his head and the veins stood out in his temples.[10]

→ **Rauschning** politician and publicist who wrote *Hitler Speaks* (1939)
→ **Chancellery** ['tʃɑ:nsələri] official home and offices of the Reich Chancellor in Berlin
→ **substantial** solid and well constructed
→ **Guderian** a German Panzer general
→ **awkwardly** ['ɔ:kwədli] without skill or grace
→ **to stoop** to carry o.'s head and shoulders bent down towards the ground
→ **jerky** ['dʒɔ:ki] sudden and uncontrolled
→ **fit of rage** a sudden feeling of wild uncontrollable anger
→ **flushed** red
→ **to hurl** (here) to shout violently
→ **accusation** [ˌækjʊ'zeɪʃən] statement charging (s.o.) with doing wrong
→ **to pop out** (of eyes) to spring out
→ **vein** [veɪn] tube that carries blood to the heart
→ **temple** one of the flattish places on each side of the forehead (Schläfe)

5. Read the following remarks about the catastrophe in Shakespearean tragedy and try to decide whether these characteristics are to be found in the final part of MACBETH. Give your reasons and illustrate your arguments when necessary.

a) In several plays Shakespeare makes here an appeal which in his time was evidently powerful: he introduces scenes of battle.[11]

b) Shakespeare very rarely makes the least attempt to surprise by his catastrophes. They are felt to be inevitable, though the precise way in which they will be brought about is not, of course, foreseen.[12]

c) In some cases Shakespeare spreads the catastrophe out, so to speak, over a considerable space, and thus shortens that difficult section which has to show the development of the counter-action. This is possible only where there is, besides the hero, some character who engages our interest in the highest degree, and with whose fate his own is bound up.[13]

Text Production ●

→ **appeal** power to move the feelings, attraction, interest
→ **evidently** clearly, plainly

→ **inevitable** impossible to prevent
→ **to bring about** to cause to happen, to produce

→ **counter-action** that part of the plot of a play in which the hero's success is destroyed by his enemies

---

9 T. L. Jarman, *The Rise and Fall of Nazi Germany.* New York: Signet Book, The New American Library, 1961, p. 299.
10 T. L. Jarman, p. 300.
11 A. C. Bradley, p. 47.
12 A. C. Bradley, p. 48.
13 A. C. Bradley, p. 49.

Act V, Scenes 6–9

Catastrophe ★

Hail, King! for so thou art. Behold, where stands Th' usurper's cursèd head: the time is free.

Why should I play the Roman fool, . . .?

Phrases for discussing the scene

Military Events

- **to draw up o.'s troops**
- to join battle (with the enemy)
- **to change sldes**
- to meet with (no/little) resistance
- **to take a castle, town, etc.**/a castle falls to the enemy

Macbeth's Reactions

- to bait a bear/bearbaiting ['beəˌbeɪtɪŋ] was a common form of amusement in the Elizabethan Age
- **courage born of despair**
- to make the final test of fate
- to be invulnerable [ɪn'vʌlnərəbəl]
- **to curse s.o. for (doing) s.th.**

Macduff's Actions

- to burn for revenge
- **to challenge s.o. (to a fight, duel, etc.)**
- to be delivered by Caesarian section [sɪˌzeərɪən 'sekʃən] (mit Kaiserschnitt entbunden werden)
- to hail s.o. king

Restoration of Order

- **to win the day/to be victorious**
- virtue is seen to triumph over evil
- order emerges out of disorder
- to shed innocent blood
- to prove o.'s manhood
- **to mourn** [mɔːn] **s.o.'s death**
- **to show o.'s gratitude to(wards) s.o.**
- to proclaim s.o. an earl
- to recall exiles ['eksaɪlz]
- **to bring s.o. to trial**

Comprehension

Unit 38

1. Retell the three scenes in your own words.
2. Scene 7, which shows one of the closing stages of Macbeth's tyranny, is marked by the final breakdown of his defence forces. Describe how this happens. ●●

Analysis

1. What is the tyrant's last illusion and how is it destroyed? ●
2. Explain the metaphor Macbeth uses at V, 7, 1–2.
3. Why, after his momentary refusal to fight, does Macbeth decide after all to face both Macduff and his own death?
4. Name some of the events that indicate that the just order is being restored. ●●
5. Is there any poetic justice in this tragedy? ➧ Poetic Justice ●●
6. What Christian ideas are present in the last four scenes of the play? ➧ Tragedy

Part III Beyond The Text

Topics for discussion

The study of MACBETH has so far been limited to a scene-by-scene analysis of the contents. Each scene was regarded as a self-contained unit and, as the scenes were read one after another, they added to our knowledge of the play, rather like a jigsaw puzzle being put together. Now that all the pieces fit and the picture is complete, we can consider the play as a whole and, indeed, the purpose of this section of the book is to offer suggestions on how MACBETH can be discussed in a broader context.

Works of literature, like any other works of art, can be looked at from different angles. Some people may be interested in the aesthetic value of a work – in the things that make it beautiful such as its form, its style or its effect; with the increasing importance of science and technology in this century, however, more and more people have become interested in the more "scientific" aspects of art and take into account such things as psychology, psycho-analysis, sociology, etc. These different angles or ways of examining a work are known in literary criticism as "approaches" and the importance or superiority of one approach over another is the subject of constant debate.

The following are intended to represent only some of the more common methods of approach used by literary critics today.

1. Approach Form

This method of approach deals with the formal aspects of a work such as genre, structure or language, without relating it in any way to things which are not part of the work itself. (work-immanence)

1.1. Why does MACBETH deserve to be classified as a tragedy? ➔ Tragedy

1.2. Analyse the structure of the play. (Before answering this, it would be useful to look again at the following questions: (Act III, Scene 3: Unit 25, Analysis (3.) and (4.). Also cf. Act I, Scene 2: Unit 3, Analysis/Text Production (7.); Act I, Scene 3: Unit 6, Analysis/Text Production (4.); Act I, Scene 6. Unit 10, Analysis/Text Production (3.); Act III, Scene 4: Unit 27, Analysis/Text Production (4.); and Act V, Scenes 4–5: Unit 37, Analysis/Text Production (5.))

1.3. Give a brief account of
a) the language and
b) the imagery
of MACBETH.

2. Approach Psychology

This approach is concerned with the characters of a literary work, their strengths and weaknesses, their emotions and the motives behind their actions. It tries to explain why the characters behave as they do and why they cannot help but meet the fate which the author has reserved for them.

2.1. Give a character description of
 a) Macbeth
 b) Lady Macbeth
 c) Banquo and Macduff
 d) Duncan and Malcolm
 e) Rosse and Lenox

2.2. Describe the reactions of the different characters of the play to Macbeth's tyranny (cf. Act IV, Scene 2: Unit 31, Analysis, 3.).

3. Approach Moral

The aim of this type of approach, which is closely linked to the Psychological Approach, is to relate the behaviour and actions of fictional characters to an agreed system of moral values. This system is always divided into two parts, into right and wrong (or virtues and vices), but because it is largely based on principles of religion and ethics, the relative importance of individual human qualities changes from generation to generation and from country to country. This system is built on abstract concepts such as pride, ambition, guilt, loyalty, etc.

3.1. Can the play be regarded as a political morality?

3.2. To what extent are Macbeth's actions directed by his own free will and to what extent are they influenced by fate (as revealed to him by the witches)?

4. Approach Sociology

This approach puts a work of art into an historical and social context. It examines the social, political and economic conditions of a given period of time and is concerned not only with the author but also with his public. There is, however, a difficulty in applying this approach to MACBETH; being a historical play, it may tell us more about the age of feudalism than about Elizabethan England.

4.1. What do we learn about the structure of feudal society in MACBETH?

Part IV: Reception of the Play

1. A note on translations

If you want to get an idea of how MACBETH was translated into German by using the resources of the German language without neglecting Shakespeare's poetic originality you may have a closer look at the following three translations of Scene 1 Act II, lines 29–64.

They were written by:

A. W. v. Schlegel and **L. Tieck** whose translation (1797–1810) of Shakespeare's plays created a German literary work of art which was to be read or to be played on the stage. With this model version of Shakespeare's work they established a Schlegel – Tieck tradition during the 19th and 20th centuries.

R. Flatter (1952–56), who rather belonged to the anti-Schlegel-Tieck tradition. Together with W. Josten he wrote quite an accurate translation into a language which was intended to be spoken on our modern stage and to be easily understood by its audience.

H. Rothe (1964), a modern translator who also tried to escape the Schlegel-Tieck tradition by writing a rather free and poetic stage-oriented translation for our modern theatre.

You may form workshop groups to compare each translation with the corresponding part of the Shakespeare original. It is advisable to consider the following general features:

- **Sounds** : alliterations, assonances, rhyme;
- **Rhythm** : kinds of feet, masculine or feminine endings of lines, enjambements or end-stopped lines;
- **Vocabulary** : poetic, modern, obsolete, colloquial etc.;
- **Metaphors** : more or less accurately translated;
- **Grammar** : word order, tenses, number, omission of words;
- **Punctuation** : changes, omissions;
- **Facts** : omissions or distortions of single facts.

Make use of your findings and show where the translator very carefully or rather carelessly adapts his translation to the Shakespeare original. Explain which of the three translations you would prefer.

1. A. W. v. Schlegel & L. Tieck[1]

MACBETH: Gute Nacht indes!
BANQUO: Dank, Herr, Euch ebenfalls!

(Banquo, Fleance und Diener ab)

MACBETH: Sag deiner Herrin, wenn mein Trank bereit,
Soll sie die Glocke ziehn. Geh du zu Bett. (Der Diener geht ab)
Ist das ein Dolch, was ich vor mir erblicke,
Der Griff mir zugekehrt? Komm, laß dich packen –
Ich fass' dich nicht, und doch seh' ich dich immer.
Bist du, Unglücksgebild, so fühlbar nicht
Der Hand, gleich wie dem Aug'? oder bist du nur
Ein Dolch der Einbildung, ein nichtig Blendwerk,
Das aus dem heiß gequälten Hirn erwächst?
Ich seh' dich noch, so greifbar von Gestalt
Wie der, den jetzt ich zücke.
Du gehst mir vor den Weg, den ich will schreiten,
Und eben solche Waffe wollt' ich brauchen.
Mein Auge ward der Narr der andern Sinne,
Oder mehr als alle wert. – Ich seh' dich stets,
Und dir an Griff und Klinge Tropfen Bluts,
Was erst nicht war. – Es ist nicht wirklich da:
Es ist die blut'ge Arbeit, die mein Auge
So in die Lehre nimmt. – Jetzt auf der halben Erde
Scheint tot Natur, und den verhangnen Schlaf
Quälen Versucherträume; Hexenkunst
Begeht den Dienst der bleichen Hekate;
Und dürrer Mord,
Durch seine Schildwacht aufgeschreckt, den Wolf,
Der ihm das Wachtwort heult, – so dieb'schen Schrittes,
Wie wild entbrannt Tarquin, dem Ziel entgegen,
Schreitet gespenstisch. –
Du festgefugte Erde, leicht verwundbar,
Hör' meine Schritte nicht, wo sie auch wandeln.
Daß nicht ausschwatzen selber deine Steine
Mein Wohinaus und von der Stunde nehmen
Den jetz'gen stummen Graus, der so ihr ziemt. –
Hier droh' ich, er lebt dort;
Für heiße Tat zu kalt das müß'ge Wort!

(Die Glocke wird angeschlagen)

Ich geh', und 's ist getan: die Glocke mahnt.
Hör' sie nicht, Duncan, 's ist ein Grabgeläut',
Das dich zu Himmel oder Höll' entbeut. (Er steigt hinauf)

2. R. Flatter[2]

MACBETH
Gute Ruh indessen!

BANQUO
Dank, Herr; das gleiche Euch.

Banquo und Fleance ab.

MACBETH
Sag deiner Herrin, wenn mein Trunk bereit ist,
Soll sie die Schelle ziehn! Du geh zu Bett!

Diener ab.

MACBETH
Ist dies ein Dolch, was ich da vor mir sehe?
Den Griff mir zugekehrt? Komm, laß dich packen!
Ich hab dich nicht, und seh dich doch – auch jetzt noch.
Unheilsgebild, bist du der Hand nicht faßbar
Wie du's dem Auge bist? Oder bist du bloß
Ein Dolch der Phantasie, ein leeres Blendwerk,
Dem Dampf entstiegen des erhitzten Hirns?
Ich seh dich doch, so deutlich in Gestalt
Wie der, den ich hier ziehe –
– zeigst mir den Weg, den gleichen, den ich gehn will –
Das gleiche Werkzeug, das ich brauchen will – –
Die Sinne äffen mir das Aug; wo nicht,
Ist es mehr wert als sie! Noch immer seh ich's –
Doch hier, an Griff und Klinge, Tropfen Bluts –
Das war vorhin noch nicht – – 's ist nichts dergleichen:
Das blutige Geschäft ist's, das sich derart
Vors Auge drängt. Nun, auf dem halben Erdrund,
Scheint Leben tot; verruchte Träume quälen
Verstohlnen Schlaf. – Hexen opfern nun
Der bleichen Hecate; und hagrer Mord,
Von seiner Schildwach aufgestört, dem Wolf,
Der seine Runde heult, – so, gleich dem Dieb,
Gleich dem Tarquin voll Schmachbegier aufs Ziel zu –
Schleicht wie ein Geist. Du festgefügter Grund,
Hör nicht, wohin mein Schreiten zielt; sonst fürcht ich,
Die Steine könnten schrei'n, worauf ich aus bin,
Und so der Welt das grause Schweigen nehmen,
Das nun geziemt. Was hilft mein Drohn? Er lebt,
Wenn Tatenglut im Hauch des Worts entschwebt.

Eine Schelle tönt.

Ich geh – so ist's getan; die Glocke ruft.
Hör sie nicht, Duncan, denn sie ist die Schelle,
Die dich zum Himmel ruft oder zur Hölle!

Ab.

3. H. Rothe[3]

MACBETH Vorläufig: gute Nacht.
BANQUO
Dank, und das Gleiche dir.
Er geht mit Fleance ab.
MACBETH
Sag deiner Herrin, wenn mein Trunk bereit ist
soll sie die Glocke ziehen. Geh du zu Bett.
Der Diener geht ab.
Ist es ein Dolch, was ich da vor mir sehe,
den Griff mir zugewandt? Komm, laß dich packen:
ich fühle dich nicht, und sehe dich trotzdem.
Wirst du, schicksalhaft Blendwerk, nicht so greifbar,
wie du mir sichtbar wirst? oder bist du
nur ein Gedankendolch, ein Wahngebilde
das aufquillt aus dem glutbedrängten Hirn?
Ich sehe dich immer noch, an Form so deutlich
wie diesen den ich zücke.
Du ziehst mich auf den Weg der vor mir liegt,
und solch ein Werkzeug halte ich bereit.
Das Auge wird zum Narren meiner Sinne,
oder beschämt sie alle: ich seh dich, seh dich;
und Griff und Klinge sind betropft mit Blut –
das war vorher nicht so. Nein, da ist nichts –
als daß der blutige Vorsatz meinen Augen
plötzlich leibhaftig wird. Jetzt scheint Natur
über dem einen Erdhalb tot, den Vorhang
des Schlafs blähen böse Träume, Hexenzunft
begeht den Kult der bleichen Hekate:
und da – von seiner Schildwacht aufgestört,
dem Wolf, der laut das Paßwort heult, rückt mit
verstohlnem Schlich, mit wollüstigem Sprung
der schrumpfige Mord geisthaft aufs Ziel.
Du festgefügte Erde, höre nicht
wohin sich meine Schritte lenken, sonst
beginnen deine Steine laut zu schwatzen,
und trennen mir das Grausen von der Stunde,
das jetzt sich zu ihr fügt. Ich drohe, und er ruht:
Worte sind Eiseshauch auf Tatenglut.
Ich gehe, dann ist es getan – *eine Glocke* die Glocke!
Duncan, höre sie nicht: dich ruft ihr Ton
zum Höllentor, oder vor Gottes Thron.

Er geht ab.

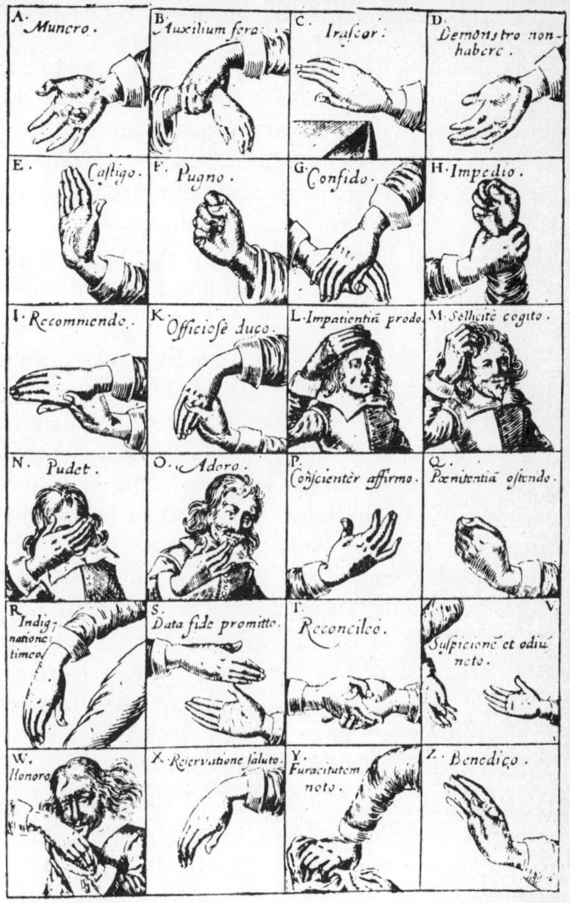

Stylized gestures for orator (John Bulwer, Chironomia, 1644)

1 August Wilhelm von Schlegel, Ludwig Tieck. *Shakespeare Sämtliche Werke Erste Abteilung/Dramatische Werke Übersetzt von August Wilhelm von Schlegel und Ludwig Tieck.* (Textgrundlage: 3. Gesamtausgabe Berlin 1843–44) Heidelberg: Lambert Schneider, 1978. p. 423ff.

2 Richard Flatter, *Shakespeare Neu übersetzt von Richard Flatter.* Wien, Bad Bocklet, Zürich. Walter Krieg Verlag. 1952. p. 253ff.

3 Hans Rothe, *William Shakespeare Dramen Vierter Band 1605–1610 In Übersetzungen und Neufassungen von Hans Rothe.* München, Wien: Albert Langen, Georg Müller, 1964, p. 33ff.

2. A note on performances

Since Shakespeare's MACBETH was first performed in the early years of the 17th century there has been little change in the text of the play. There has, however, been an enormous change in the way the play has been presented; not only have countless generations of actors impersonated its characters but there have also been great changes in the conditions and concepts of the stage. And, last but not least, each epoch has had its own audience and, if stage directors wanted to be successful, they had to take into account the ideas, tastes and expectations of their particular audience.

A literary text like Shakespeare's MACBETH does not offer the actor or his audience historical truth. It contains a number of facts drawn from a person's life which, together with material invented by the author, form a reality existing in the text only. The actor is expected to interpret and re-create this reality on the stage with the help of words, actions, gestures and so on. His audience is invited to follow the actor's actions and to create his imagined world within its own mind. Although the words of the text do not change, they offer innumerable possibilities of establishing and interpreting an imaginary world depending, for example, on an actor's ability or on his audience's interests. This is eminently true of MACBETH, the text of which offers many different ways of creating its imaginary world. It has allowed stage directors of widely differing epochs to set the scene and to portray the characters, even the minor ones, as they saw fit. In this way each age also helped to characterize itself and set the task of re-interpreting the text for the following generations.

The following passage from M. Rosenberg's book *The Masks of Macbeth* (Berkeley: University of California Press, 1978, p. 222f.) gives an idea of how four lines of the text may be interpreted in completely different ways. The four lines are Lady Macbeth's invocation of the evil spirits in Act I, Scene 5 (ll. 38–41):

> . . . Come, you, spirits
> That tend on mortal thoughts, unsex me here,
> And fill me, from the crown to the toe, top-full
> Of direst cruelty! . . .

The lady may perform enough of a magic ritual to emphasize a link with witchcraft or demonism: thus Krahl with her toe, drew a magic circle about herself before beginning, and stood in its center, straddle-legged, impudent. The other side of demon worship is blasphemy, and this has sometimes been stipulated. Bergman's (1944) Lady invoked possession while standing under the image, dominating her room, of a bleeding Christ. A Czech Lady knelt in the familiar posture of genuflection, and prayed to murdering ministers. Rosemary Murphy, wearing a gown slit from neck to pelvis so as almost to bare her breasts, also began as if to pray – then suddenly ripped off the crucifix, spat on it, and threw it away. Rigg, rigid, pale-faced, tight-lipped, deliberately turned her crucifix upside down, as noted, spat over it, as a kind of implied contract with the demonic. Mirren objectified this implication by using her small dagger to draw blood from her arm; then she acted as if she were initiating a seance

→ **straddle-legged** standing with one's legs wide apart
→ **impudent** showing no respect
→ **blasphemy** ['blæsfəmi] the use of disrespectful language when speaking about God
→ **to stipulate** to demand (as a condition)
→ **to invoke** to call out (to s.o., especially God or spirits) for help
→ **genuflection** [ˌdʒenʊ'flekʃən] the act of bending one's knees as a sign of religious respect
→ **pelvis** basin-shaped bones at the base of the body (Becken)
→ **to rip off** to tear away quickly
→ **to objectify s.th.** so turn s.th. abstract into s.th. concrete
→ **to initiate** to begin

– with gestures that her Macbeth, Williamson, would echo at Come, sealing night . . . (III, II, 56)

What it could mean to Lady Macbeth to invite so terrible an unholiness is suggested by Sheila Allen: "I believe she is frightened and doubtful of pulling off the killing – hence the passion and despair of 'Come you spirits.'" Dench made anguish visual. She could almost be seen thinking what she said was in her mind: "Dare I? Just for this once?" Then she slowly knelt, in a circle of light, her hands outstretched, pointing forward and down. Only after a deep, strained breath could she find strength to begin; and as the first words came from her she became more and more frightened at what she was doing. When she reached topfull/Of direst cruelty, she could not bear any more: terrified, she broke off, and fled back into the darkness. Only slowly did she regain enough resolution to return and complete, fearfully, the summoning.

General to Lady Macbeth's characterization is a crux which every critic and actor must confront: what change, if any, must take place in her to make her what she becomes – murderess, and after. For the Terrible Woman, the invocation is less a plea for conversion than for enlargement: strengthen me to do what I want to do. She may speak to the spirits almost as if they are kin; she and they understand each other, may have held commerce before. To the tender Loving Wife, at the other extreme, the call to the supernatural is a desperate, painful, frightened appeal to strange powers for the only kind of strength that might enable her to sustain her new intent – a strength that must end in frightful weakness. Ranging between these poles, Lady Macbeth's polyphony sounds many subtle chords, of mingled ferocity and tenderness, ambition for self and ambition for husband, murderous determination that may be achieved by strenuous suppression of scruple and fear.

→ **to pull off** to succeed (in doing s.th. which is difficult)
crux [ʌ] the most difficult part or the most critical point (of s.th.)
→ **plea** call, appeal
→ **kin** member of the same family
→ **commerce** ['--] (here) communication
→ **polyphony** [pəˈlɪfəni] quality of having many different sounds or voices
→ **chord** [kɔːd] (mus.) Akkord
→ **mingled** mixed, combined
→ **ferocity** [fəˈrɒsətɪ] quality of being cruel and violent
→ **strenuous** needing great effort

Study Helps:

Hilde Krahl	German actress who impersonated Lady Macbeth at the Volkstheater, Vienna in 1959
Rosemary Murphy	American actress performing in New York in 1973
Diana Rigg	British actress performing in 1972/73
Helen Mirren	British actress performing in 1974/75
Nicol Williamson	British actor who played Macbeth in 1974/75
Sheila Allen	British actress performing in 1968, 1973 and 1976
Judi Dench	British actress performing in 1976

Part V: Glossary of Literary Terms

ACTION ['ækʃən] . . . 'the actual and total process of doing sth., which takes some time to be completed'.[1] When used in connection with a play the word refers to the main events of it, the complex chain of single incidents which are linked together by chronological, accidental, and causal connections. Thus action supplies the material for ➧ PLOT, in which the separate elements are linked with the help of the principle of cause and effect. Action is one basic element of ➧ DRAMA. There is a difference between (1) INTERNAL or PSYCHOLOGICAL ACTION, which deals with the development of feelings, thoughts, and ideas, and (2) EXTERNAL ACTION, which has largely to do with events observed outside the mind.

ALLEGORY ['æləgəri] A story or passage whose setting, characters, and action have an indirect as well as a direct meaning. There are two possible kinds of allegory: (1) POLITICAL or HISTORICAL ALLEGORY, which deals with historically or politically important persons or events; and (2) ALLEGORIES of a PHILOSOPHICAL, MORAL, or RELIGIOUS kind, which illustrate or teach a principle or a set of ideas and beliefs, and in which abstract powers or ideas or character traits are personified.[2] Also ➧ PERSONIFICATION. The personifications in MACBETH belong to the second type of allegory: Fortune (I,2,14), Valour (I,2,19), Justice (I,2,29), Fate (I,5,27), etc.

ALLITERATION [əˌlɪtə'reɪʃən] The repetition of identical consonant sounds, usually at the beginning of two or more neighbouring words, in order to give special stress to ideas or to pictures in words (➧ IMAGES) which are more heard than seen. Also ➧ ASSONANCE. Example: **F**air is **f**oul . . . **f**og and **f**ilthy air (I,1,10, f.).

ALLUSION [ə'lu:ʒən] An indirect reference to something, e.g. to a well-known event in history or literature (thus when at I,2,41 the bleeding captain mentions 'Golgotha' we think of the crucifixion and 'the place of a skull'); or to people or events of the author's own time. Thus the porter's thoughts about the 'equivocator' (II,3,7 ff.) are related to the trial of Father Garnet in 1606 for his part in the Gunpowder Plot, an alleged attempt to blow up the King and Parliament the previous year. This Jesuit had said that equivocation, i.e. the telling of a lie after one has solemnly promised to tell the truth, was sometimes justified if it was done for a good reason.

AMBIGUITY [ˌæmbə'gju:əti] A word or a phrase which may reasonably be interpreted in two or more different ways and does not give us any help when we try to decide which of the different interpretations is the true or correct one. Poetic language is characterized by deliberate ambiguity, for in poetry phrases are often given more than one meaning in order to increase their beauty or the richness of ideas linked with them. Ambiguity can also be used to avoid committing or compromising oneself (as is done by Macbeth at II,1,25).

ANALOGY [ə'nælədʒi] A comparison, stated or implied, between two objects which resemble each other in certain respects. A ➧ SIMILE is an explicit analogy, whereas in the case of a ➧ METAPHOR the analogy is merely implied.

ANAPAEST ['ænəpi:st] One of the kinds of metrical ➧ FOOT. It consists of two unstressed or weakly-stressed syllables and one strongly-stressed syllable. Example: '. . . I am young' (IV,3,14).

ANAPHORA [ə'næfərə] A literary or ➧ RHETORICAL DEVICE consisting of the repetition of a word or phrase in successive lines or clauses. Example: the repeated use of the word 'Though' in Macbeth's speech to the witches at IV,1,50–61.

ANTAGONIST [æn'tægənəst] The character in a play who most actively opposes the hero or ➧ PROTAGONIST, whom he fights or rivals. Example: Macduff.

1 E. Werlich, *Wörterbuch der Text-Interpretation.* Dortmund: Lensing, 1969. p. 97.
2 M. H. Abrams, *A Glossary of Literary Terms.* New York: Holt, Rinehardt and Winston, Inc. 1981 repr. p. 4f.

ANTITHESIS [æn'tɪθəsɪs] A ➧ RHETORICAL DEVICE involving the placing together of two opposite ideas, words, or phrases. This contrast of meaning forms a kind of balance of ideas which is often underlined by their position in grammatical structures of the same kind. Also ➧ PARALLELISM. Example: 'look like the innocent flower|But be the serpent under't.' (I,5,64f.).

APOSTROPHE [ə'pɒstrəfi] A Type of ➧ RHETORICAL DEVICE (also ➧ FIGURES OF SPEECH) in which a person directly addresses an object, some abstract quality, another person (often absent or dead), or some supernatural power. It often expresses the deepest feelings of the speaker. Example: 'Thou sure and firm-set earth,|Hear 'not my steps . . .' (II,1,56f.).

APRON STAGE [ˌeɪprən'steɪdʒ] A stage with an 'apron' (i.e. that part of the stage which juts out into the audience). This was one of the characteristic features of the Elizabethan playhouse, in which the audience surrounded the stage on three sides.

ASIDE [ə'saɪd] ➧ MONOLOGUE

ASSONANCE ['æsənəns] The repetitions of the same or similar vowel sounds in the stressed syllables of neighbouring words. The device may be used to create sound effects or to stress or repeat a particular idea. Example: 'When shall **we** thr**ee** m**ee**t again . . .?' (I,1,1,).

ASYNDETON [æ'sɪndɪtən] The omission of conjunctions. Example: 'But now I am cabined, cribbed, confined, bound in|To saucy doubts and fears.' (III,4,24f.).

ATMOSPHERE ['ætməsfɪəʳ] Used in connection with a literary work. This refers to the author's attitude to his theme (➧MOOD) and audience (➧TONE), and to the particular emotional and moral background with which he surrounds the characters, places, and objects that he is dealing with. All this has an effect on the audience: on their feelings of calm or unrest, of hope or fear, of good or evil. This 'atmosphere' is something that the author builds up gradually. Example: the key-words in Duncan's and Banquo's speeches about Macbeth's castle at I,6,1–10.

ATTITUDINAL ADVERB [ˌætɪtjuːdɪnəl'ædvɜːb] An adverb expressing the speaker's degree of certainty or doubt about what is said, or his attitude towards the value or degree of importance of what is said.[3] Example: with a heightening effect: 'Things have been **strangely** borne.' – With a heightening and ironical effect: 'Banquo walked **too** late . . .' (III,6,3 and 5).

BLANK VERSE [ˌblæŋk'vɜːs] This consists of unrhymed lines (➧RHYME) with ten syllables each, and stresses on the second, fourth, sixth, eighth, and tenth syllables (iambic pentameter). These stresses are sometimes irregularly placed, however, and the main internal pauses (➧CAESURA) occur at different points in the different lines. Moreover, sentence structure and sense need not be completed at the end of a line (➧ END-STOPPED LINE), for both may be continued in the following lines (➧ RUN-ON LINE). In this way passages of verse that are quite complex in both form and content can be built up. Thus in Shakespeare's hand blank verse becomes an instrument of considerable flexibility.

CAESURA [sɪː'zjʊərə] A noticeable pause in the regular rhythm and movement of a line of verse. Such pauses show how normal speech movement influences the verse and prevents its regular rhythmical flow from having full control of the movement of the line. The caesura may occur anywhere in the line, usually between the foot and the next, and often near the middle of the line. There may be as many as two or three caesuras in one line.

CATASTROPHE [kə'tæstrəfi] The final stage in the ➧ FALLING ACTION of a tragedy. It marks the winding-up of the ➧ PLOT, with the tragic failure and death of the hero. In Shakespeare's tragedies the catastrophe usually extends over the full length of the 5th act. Sometimes it is

3 E. Werlich, *A Text Grammar of English.* Heidelberg: Quelle & Meyer, 1976. p. 276/277.

marked by battle scenes, by a final presentation of some of the hero's nobler qualities and by a brief glimmer of false hope for his escape from the inevitable destruction that awaits him.

CHARACTER ['kærəktəʳ] One of the people in a play, etc., possessing certain qualities of mind and moral nature which are presented through dialogue and description. These characteristics may be (1) related to a single dominant idea capable of being summarized in a few words: this produces a 'FLAT' CHARACTER or TYPE; or else (2) they may form a complex character with contradictory or surprising features and plenty of detail serving to build up a picture of a life-like individual: this produces a 'ROUND' CHARACTER. – A character may be STATIC (i.e. fixed) or stable if he does not change in any way in the course of the play, or DYNAMIC if for some reason he does develop or change.

CHARACTERIZATION [ˌkærəktəraɪ'zeɪʃən] An author's way of presenting his characters. If characterization is really effective the audience will be almost persuaded that the characters presented are real people whose lives go on after the play is over. (1) In EXPLICIT CHARACTERIZATION the motives or qualities of a character's mind and moral nature are fully described and often also evaluated (a) by the character himself (SELF-ANALYSIS) in dialogue or monologue, (b) in a CHARACTER PORTRAYAL by another character; or (c) by the dramatist himself in the ➧ STAGE DIRECTIONS. (2) In IMPLICIT CHARACTERIZATION a character's mind and moral nature, his behaviour and social background, etc. are represented not by means of this kind of direct description or evaluation but by showing (a) the character's outer appearance, his social, economic, or his cultural background, and (b) his gestures, habits, and facial expressions, his speeches and actions, and his purposes and ideas on the stage (DRAMATIC CHARACTERIZATION). (c) A character may also be presented from within his mind by showing the content and movement of his consciousness (his memories, sense impressions, and imaginings) by means of both ➧ MONOLOGUE and ➧ DIALOGUE (INTROSPECTIVE CHARACTERIZATION).

CHORUS ['kɔːrəs] In Greek tragedy this was a group of men of lower social status than the main characters in whose fate they were interested. Like ordinary people whose feelings of fear, sorrow, and love are moved, this chorus – generally in response to particular events on the stage – mainly commented on the action of the play, representing common-sense, or conservative moral, religious, or social views. Even though there was no formal chorus in Elizabethan drama choric comment was occasionally used. Thus a single (choral) character sometimes introduced a play or the separate acts (Prologue), or spoke an Epilogue. Such a character could also express an author's comments on the play or an additional character's view of the world presented. Example: In IV,3 Macduff and Malcolm perform a choral function.

CLIMAX ['klaɪmæks] The moment when we (the audience) react most intensely (➧ TENSION) to the action of the play. As the moment of our greatest emotional interest in the play it is often identical with the ➧ CRISIS, the point at which the protagonist's success (➧ RISING ACTION) begins to change into failure (➧ FALLING ACTION). 'However, CRISIS is used exclusively in the sense of STRUCTURE, whereas **climax** is used as a synonym for CRISIS **and** as a description of the intensity of interest in the reader or spectator.[4] Example: In MACBETH crisis and climax are not identical, as the crisis occurs at the escape of Fleance (III,3), while the climax is the banquet scene (III,4).

COMIC RELIEF [ˌkɒmɪk rɪ'liːf] 'The use of humorous characters, speeches, or scenes in a serious or tragic work, especially a dramatic work. Such elements were almost universal in Elizabethan tragedy.'[5]

4 C. H. Holman, *A Handbook to Literature.* Indianapolis: Odyssey Press, 1973, 3rd edition, p. 102.
5 M. C. Abrams, p. 28.

CONFLICT ['kɒnflɪkt] This is the element that controls and decides the ➧ ACTION of a play. Conflict means a struggle of opposing ideas, beliefs or forces, including the struggle between the hero (➧ PROTAGONIST) of the play and someone else (➧ ANTAGONIST), or his struggle with something inside or outside himself. There must be a cause, a convincing reason for this conflict. There must also be some aim behind the struggle between the opposing forces. The events marking this struggle form the ➧ PLOT. '**Conflict** is the raw material out of which PLOT is constructed.'[6] The conflict may take different forms: (1) the struggle of the protagonist against someone else, usually the antagonist. These two figures may stand for different religious, moral, political, or social values. (2) The protagonist may fight against the power of nature. (3) He may be in conflict with the forces of society, or (4) there may be a struggle between opposing values and conflicting desires within the protagonist's mind.

CONSONANCE ['kɒnsənəns] Repetition of final consonants in stressed syllables whose vowel sounds are, however, not identical. Example: hea**th** – Macbe**th** (I,1,6/7).

COUPLET ['kʌplɪ̈t] A pair of rhyming lines, usually of the same length. The lines usually have eight or ten syllables each. Example: Hecate's words at III,5,2–35.

CRISIS ['kraɪsɪ̈s] 'The point at which the opposing forces that create the CONFLICT interlock in the decisive action on which the PLOT will turn.'[7] From this point onwards the ➧ PROTAGONIST'S position will either become better (after having been bad), or it will become worse (after having been good). 'Crisis' is a term characterizing the structure of a play and its plot. It often coincides with the ➧ CLIMAX, the point of the greatest emotional reaction on the part of the audience. This is not the case with MACBETH, however, for the crisis occurs in III,3, with the escape of Fleance, whereas the banquet scene (III,4) marks the climax of the play.

DACTYL ['dæktɪl] dactylic [dæk'tɪlɪk] One of the standard feet (➧ FOOT) in traditional meter. It consists of one stressed syllable followed by two unstressed syllables. Example: '**p**rocreant cradle' (I,6,8).

DIALOGUE ['daɪəlɒg] Written or spoken conversation between two or more characters, performed by actors on the stage. It is not only the characters' actions but also their conversation that helps to develop the plot of a play (and the conflict that is the raw material of this), by showing the interaction of people and of ideas. Dialogue also serves to inform us about the speakers' minds and moral natures, their interests, social background, etc. In drama dialogue is often in verse, although Elizabethan plays use prose in comic scenes or with people of lower social status. Dramatic dialogue is mostly more correct and precise than in real life, avoiding the repetitions, false starts, and the grammatical mistakes that are characteristic of everyday conversation. The speeches making up the dialogue are often longer, using more rhetorical, more carefully worked-out language; this is especially true of Elizabethan plays.

DRAMA ['drɑːmə] The general term for stage plays. Drama has some organizing principles, which, however, are not always followed in modern plays: (1) It is based on a main **story**, on a series of human actions presented in chronological **order**. (2) To make sense, these actions have to be linked by the **principle of cause and effect**. Thus a 'story' is changed into a **plot**. (3) Drama deals with human actions and with the interplay of opposing groups or persons. **Conflict**, 'the struggle which grows out of the interplay of the two opposing forces in a PLOT',[8] provides the building-material for the construction of a plot. (4) Drama shows how action, conflict, and plot develop. By means of dialogue and plot it must try to show how cause is followed by effect, and

6 C. H. Holman, p. 119.
7 C. H. Holman, p. 129.
8 C. H. Holman, p. 118.

how a particular action or decision brings forth a particular reaction. This means that in most plays action, conflict and plot are shown as taking place **in the present** and influencing the **future**. Drama thus generally presents some kind of human interaction as actually going on as one watches. (5) Drama is performed by **actors** who impersonate the characters with suitable gestures, action, dialogue, etc., for the benefit of the audience: 'drama, as an art form, looks towards immediate physical representation on the stage.'[9] Drama requires an **audience**. Although the text of a play does not change after publication, the other elements of drama are subject to change. These **variable factors** are: the actors, the theatre and its stage, and the audiences of each successive period, to whom the dramatic conflict, plot, and ideas have to appeal.

DRAMATIC FUNCTION is the special purpose of particular elements or passages (character, action, dialogue, scene, etc.) within the framework of a play. Thus a character may serve to create an element of ➧ CONFLICT, or to act as a foil to another character; a new development in the action may set a subplot or a new conflict in motion; a particular dialogue may contribute richness and psychological depth to the character portrayal, or introduce a new element of conflict; a particular scene in the play may help to increase the tension, may provide ➧ COMIC RELIEF, or may set the ➧ FALLING ACTION, CATASTROPHE, etc., in motion.

DRAMATIC IRONY [drə'mætɪk'aɪərəni] In many cases this is identical with **tragic** irony. A dramatic effect in which the words or acts of a character or characters are understood in two different ways by two different audiences. In a particular dramatic situation a character may say or do something which he and the characters he addresses may only understand according to its importance as it appears to them; they are ignorant of future events. The spectators, however, who form the second audience and who know about future developments, realize that the character is completely unaware of his actual situation. They share this knowledge with the author of the play. Thus they interpret the words and deeds of the ignorant characters quite differently from the characters themselves, connecting them with tragic (or sometimes comical) consequences for the characters. This contrast between the characters' ignorance and the spectators' foreknowledge creates a dramatic irony, a moment of heightened interest, horror, pity, satisfaction or relief for the audience. Example: Duncan's statements at I,4,11–14; 16–19; 56–58.

DRAMATIC [drə'mætɪk] Of or related to drama.

DRAMATIC STRUCTURE OF TRAGEDY The framework of a play may be recognized first of all by simply following its mechanical division into acts or scenes. Any deeper analysis, however, will try to show the development of dramatic ➧ CONFLICT and ➧ PLOT. Some critics believe that the five-act structure of the tragedy corresponds more or less closely to the five main steps of the dramatic action: ➧ EXPOSITION, ➧ RISING ACTION, ➧ CRISIS/CLIMAX, ➧ FALLING ACTION, and ➧ CATASTROPHE. But in fact such a strict structural interpretation cannot be applied literally to any Elizabethan or Jacobean play.

DRAMATIS PERSONAE [ˌdræmətɪ̈s pɜː'səʊnaɪ] The characters in a play. Also: an explanatory list of these persons at the beginning of a printed play.

ELISION [ɪ'lɪʒən] The leaving-out of a sound at the end of a word in order to create a regular effect in ➧ VERSE and its ➧ RHYTHM. In English verse this is usually marked by an apostrophe [ə'pɒstrəfi]. Example: '. . . If **'t** be so, . . .' (III,1,63).

ELLIPSIS [ɪ'lɪpsɪ̈s] The leaving-out of one or more words which are necessary to complete a grammatical structure, but which can be easily understood and added to the surrounding words by the listener or reader. Example: 'I see thee still;/And on thy blade and dudgeo**n g**outs of blood' (II,1,45).

9 T. J. Shipley, *Dictionary of World Literature.* Totowa, New Jersey: Littlefield, Adams & Co: 1968, 2nd edition, p. 106.

EMPHASIS ['emfəsɪs] Special force given to those words or ideas within a passage which are thought to be important. In speech this may be done by lowering or raising one's voice or by stressing a particular word. In writing emphasis can be achieved by (1) using **striking arrangements of sounds:** ➧ ALLITERATION, ➧ ASSONANCE; (2) **using rare words;** example: 'no **jutty**, frieze,/Buttress, nor **coign** of vantage, but this bird . . .' (I,6,6–7) or ➧ RHYMING JINGLE: Example: 'hurlyburly' (I,1,3); (3) **using unusual phrases;** Example 'his pendant bed, and procreant cradle' (1,6,8); (4) **using an unusual word order;** e.g. the TRANSFERRED EPITHET, which refers to a noun which it does not logically describe; Example: 'the air|Nimbly and sweetly recommends itself|Unto our **gentle** senses.' (I,6,1–3); (5) **varying the sentence order,** e.g. by using Inversion (I,4,32f.); Interruption (V,3,19); Repetition (I,3,130f.); (6) **stressing the important idea** e.g. by the use of Epithets; Example 'my black and deep desires' (I,4,51) and of Contrast; Example: 'Words to the heat of deeds too cold breath gives.' (II,1,61).

END-STOPPED LINE A line in which grammatical structure and sense are completed at the end. Examples: I,1,1–4.

ENJAMBEMENT [ɪn'dʒæmmənt] This is a technical term for what occurs when grammatical structure and sense are not completed at the end of a line, but are carried on in the following one. Examples: II,1,36/37; 37/38.

ENUMERATION [ɪˌnjuːmə'reɪʃən] A ➧ FIGURE OF SPEECH in which things or characteristics included within the same general idea are listed. Example: 'I grant him bloody,|Luxurious, avaricious, false, deceitful,|Sudden, malicious, smacking of every sin|That has a name' (IV,3,57–60).

EUPHEMISM ['juːfəmɪzəm] A ➧ FIGURE OF SPEECH ➧ in which an unpleasant word or evil term is replaced by a milder term that does not cause disgust, shock, or fear in other people. This is done for reasons of strategy in communication in order to hide the unpleasant reality, either to spare people's feelings or to deceive them. Example: the use of the word 'business' in order to avoid the word 'murder' (I,5,66; I,7,31; II,1,48; III,1,123).

EPITHET ['epɪθet] A word or word group suggesting colours, sounds, etc., serving to illustrate or stress a particular characteristic of a person or object, etc. Examples: adjective: 'his stealthy pace' (II,1,54); noun + participle: 'temple-haunting martlet' (I,6,4); adjective + adverb + participle: 'sure and firm-set earth' (II,1,56). Also: 'Transferred Epithet' under ➧ EMPHASIS (5).

EXCITING FORCE [ɪk'saɪtɪŋˌfɔːs] A structural term referring to the character, situation, or event that gives rise to the ➧ CONFLICT in a play and sets the ➧ RISING ACTION in motion. Examples: the witches' prophecies in I,3 stir up the protagonist's ambition and so encourage him to begin making his evil plans to kill the king and seize the crown.

EXCLAMATION [ˌeksklə'meɪʃən] A ➧ FIGURE OF SPEECH: a complete or incomplete utterance (➧ INTERJECTION) expressing sudden strong feeling, such as shock or surprise. Examples: a full statement beginning with an Interjection: 'O! never|Shall sun that morrow see!' (I,5,59); an Ellipsis: 'We fail!' (I,7,59).

EXPOSITION [ˌekspə'zɪʃən] A Structural term with the same meaning as INTRODUCTION. The first part of a play, establishing the ➧ TONE and helping to establish the ➧ ATMOSPHERE. In the exposition the time and place in which the play is set, are established, some of the characters are presented, and some information is given about the events that are supposed to have happened before the action of the play begins. The expositions of Shakespeare's tragedies are masterly. They begin with short, startling scenes which arouse the spectators' interest and capture their attention for the longer, more explanatory scene that follows.

EYE RHYME ➧ RHYME

FALLING ACTION That part of the dramatic plot of a tragedy which follows the ➔ CLIMAX and marks the beginning of the second half of the play, showing the advance of the ➔ Antagonist and the forces opposing the ➔ PROTAGONIST. Also ➔ TRAGIC FORCE.

FIGURATIVE LANGUAGE [ˌfɪgjʊrətɪv' læŋgwɪdʒ] 'Intentional departure from the normal order, construction, or meaning of words in order to gain strength and freshness of expression, to create a pictorial effect, to describe by ANALOGY, or to discover and illustrate similarities in otherwise dissimilar things.'[10] ➔ ANALOGY; ➔ FIGURES OF SPEECH.

FIGURATIVE MEANING [ˌfɪgjʊrətɪv'miːnɪŋ] A word usually has a normal or generally-accepted concrete sense which may be regarded as its matter-of-fact or **literal** meaning. In the course of time or in poetic language such a word may be used in some additional or figurative sense that creates an unexpected picture or comparison. In many cases this **figurative** meaning has been taken over from another word, to whose original or literal meaning it more properly belongs. Example: the seeds of plants are concrete objects but become an abstract idea in the phrase 'the seeds of time' (I,3,58).[11]

FIGURES OF SPEECH ['fɪgəz əv'spiːtʃ] A general term for a whole class of uses of language which are comparatively uncommon in everyday language but frequent in ➔ FIGURATIVE LANGUAGE, in which the literal meaning of words is changed in order to 'make a meaning appear fresher, stronger, or more complex, to create a sensory effect through stylistic techniques, or to widen the reference of a word or expression'.[12] Figures of speech fall into two main groups: (1) **Rhetorical devices,** which are deviations or noticeable departures from the normal word-order, usage, etc. Although the basic meaning of the words is unchanged, special force is given to the ideas expressed (➔ EMPHASIS; ➔ ENUMERATION; ➔ RHETORICAL QUESTION). Special effects, e.g. of sound and rhythm, are also possible (➔ ANAPHORA). (2) **Tropes** [trəʊps], in which there is a 'turn' or alteration of the basic meaning of a word. In a typical trope a word is used with a ➔ FIGURATIVE MEANING which has somehow been transferred to it from the literal meaning of another word. There are four main kinds of trope: ➔ IMAGE; ➔ SYMBOL; ➔ SIMILE; ➔ METAPHOR.

FOOT [fʊt] The combination of a strong stress and a weak stress or stresses which forms the regularly-repeated metric unit of a line of verse. "The relatively stronger-stressed syllable is called, for short, 'stressed'; the relatively weaker-stressed syllables are called 'light', or 'slack' or simply 'unstressed'."[13], ➔ IAMBUS; ANAPAEST; TROCHEE; DACTYL. A line of verse – made up of feet, with their regular pattern of stressed and unstressed elements – is named according to the number of feet it contains: **monometer** [mə'nɒmɪtəʳ] = one foot; dimeter ['dɪmɪtəʳ] = two feet; **trimeter** ['trɪmɪtəʳ] = three feet; **tetrameter** [te'træmɪtəʳ] = four feet; **pentameter** [pen'tæmɪtəʳ] = five feet; **hexameter** [hek'sæmɪtəʳ] = six feet; etc.

FORESHADOWING [fɔː'ʃædəʊɪŋ] A narrative element of drama which occurs when a character 'anticipates and reports what the outcome of the whole play, or some part of it, will be'.[14] Example: Hecate at III,5,26 ff.

GROUND [graʊnd] That part of an ➔ ANALOGY which is the basis of the comparison, whether explicit (➔ SIMILE) or implicit (➔ METAPHOR) in ➔ FIGURATIVE LANGUAGE. The ground is the connecting set of ideas to be found (a) in the literal meaning of the poet's subject (➔ TENOR) in a Simile or Metaphor and (b) in the figurative meaning or object which illustrates it (➔ VEHICLE) by

10 C. H. Holman, p. 223.
11 Rotter/Bendl, *Your Companion To English Texts.* München: Manz Verlag, 1978, p. 133 f.
12 T. L. Lemon, *A Glossary For The Study of English.* New York, London, Toronto: Oxford University Press, 1971. p. 71.
13 M. H. Abrams, p. 94.
14 R. Scholes, C. H. Klaus, *Elements of Drama.* London: New York, London, Toronto, Oxford University Press, 1971, p. 22.

drawing attention to it. Example: the Simile at I,2,7ff. 'Doubtful (= Ground) it (= Tenor; here: 'battle') stood, As two spent swimmers, that do cling together|And choke their art.' (Vehicle = from 'As two . . .' to '. . . their art'.)

HEXAMETER [hek'sæmətəʳ] ➧ FOOT.

HYPERBOLE [haɪ'pɜːbəli] A ➧ FIGURE OF SPEECH in which an obvious overstatement or exaggerated statement is made without any attempt to make the listener believe it is true. Example: 'All the perfumes of Arabia | will not sweeten this little hand' (V,1,40f.). See also II,2,59–62.

IAMB(US) – IAMBIC [aɪ'æmbəs; aɪ'æmbɪk] One of the standard types of ➧ FOOT in traditional ➧ METRE. It consists of an unstressed syllable followed by a stressed one. Example: 'If **I** say **s**ooth, I m**u**st rep**o**rt they **w**ere.' (I,2,36).

IMAGE ['ɪmɪdʒ] A ➧ FIGURE OF SPEECH, more precisely a ➧ TROPE, calling up in our minds the picture of a real object or concrete action which we can almost see, hear, touch, taste or smell. An image serves to make an impression more vivid and definite, and is 'a literal and concrete representation' of a sense impression or of 'an object that can be known by one or more of the senses'.[15] Example: 'With his **brandished** steel,|Which **smoked** with **bloody** execution,' (I,2,17–18).

INTENSIFYING ADVERB [ɪn'tensɪfaɪɪŋ 'ædvɜːb] An adverb that has 'a heightening or lowering effect on some unit in the sentence'.[16] Such an adverb expresses the qualitative or quantitative degree of an action or the intensity of the emotional effect that a particular event creates within a spectator's mind. Example: 'Thou playedst most foully for't' (III,1,3).

INTERLUDE ['ɪntəluːd] One of the plays (some of which were dialogues with only two characters), thought to have been used to entertain banqueters, or else performed between two other, longer plays, or in the intervals of a single long play, in the 15th and 16th centuries. Interludes usually showed the rough and noisy behaviour of clownish characters, or contained witty dialogues intended not only to amuse the audience but also to criticize religious, political, or social groups and attitudes.

INTERJECTION [ˌɪntə'dʒekʃən] A phrase, word, or group of sounds used as a sudden remark, usually expressing a shock of surprise and astonishment or some other pleasant or unpleasant feeling. Examples: '**Marry,** he was dead' (III,6,4); 'All the perfumes of Arabia|will not sweeten this little hand. **Oh! oh! oh!**' (V,1,40f.).

INVERSION [ɪn'vɜːʃən] The use of a word-order opposite to the normal one. Thus a sentence or phrase is made to begin with what would normally be the last word: it goes from the end to the beginning. This is dome for reasons of stress (➧ EMPHASIS) or to make the verse run more smoothly. Examples: Object before the verb: '**My noble partner**|You greet with present grace' (I,3,54f.) adjective after the noun: 'to speak things **strange**' (I,2,48).

INVOCATION [ˌɪnvə'keɪʃən] An address to a superior being or force (God, the Muses, Nature, the stars, etc.) linked with an appeal for assistance or inspiration. Examples: Come, you spirits,|That tend on mortal thoughts, unsex me here . . .' (I,5,38f.). See also I,4,50ff.; II,1,56ff.; and II,1,7ff.

IRONY ['aɪərəni] ➧ VERBAL IRONY; ➧ DRAMATIC IRONY.

LEITMOTIF ['laɪtməʊˌtiːf] Originally a musical theme associated with a particular person, feeling or object. In literary criticism the term is often applied to the repeated appearance of a characteristic word or phrase, or a significant description, situation, or idea in a literary text. The repeated

15 C. H. Holman, p. 263.
16 E. Werlich, 1976, p. 278.

appearance of such important thought units or phrases of special meaning brings them before us again and again, thus creating a certain unifying effect within the text. Example: 'Fair is foul, and foul is fair' (I,1,10). Other leitmotifs in MACBETH include the ➧ IMAGERY of sleep, clothing and milk as the most basic life-giving food, the idea of growth in nature, and disease, and the theme of feudal honour and duty contrasted with equivocation and treachery. The symbolic battle between light and darkness is another of the play's leitmotifs.

LITERAL MEANING ['lɪtərəl 'mi:nɪŋ] The matter-of-fact, normal, generally accepted sense of a word or phrase, based upon what is actually said or written. If we concentrate too much on the literal sense, however, we are 'apt to miss the real spirit and meaning'.[17]

MESSENGER'S REPORT ['mesəndʒez rɪ'pɔ:t] Rather like the Greek ➧ CHORUS, the messenger's report is a narrative technique in which events or actions are not shown on the stage but are merely related or described. Sometimes there is even a second messenger whose report continues the narrated events and may give them added plausibility by repetition. Example: the bleeding captain's and Rosse's reports on the battle (I,2,7 ff. and 50 ff.).

METAPHOR ['metəfəʳ] A ➧ FIGURE OF SPEECH: one of the tropes. Example: . . . 'my gashes cry for help' (I,2,43). A metaphor is an indirectly-expressed comparison calling attention to the similarity or ➧ ANALOGY between two otherwise dissimilar objects by giving to the first (here the bleeding captain's wounds or gashes) some quality of the second (here a wide open shouting mouth). The poet looks at the first object (the wounds) with a kind of 'double vision'[18]: at one and the same time he makes us see the object in a literal, concrete and practical way (we see the wounds as real), grasping the basic idea of it (➧TENOR), and makes us think of it in a pictorial or figurative way (➧VEHICLE) that reveals a more unusual meaning, so that we see the object in an unaccustomed and imaginative light (as a wide open, shouting mouth). Tenor and Vehicle together make up a metaphor. They are linked by common ideas and associations, the ➧ GROUND of the analogy which must be discovered by careful analysis. In our example the captain's open wounds which urgently require seeing to resemble a red mouth crying for help. Among the resemblances here are those of colour, urgency and a sense of danger.

METRE ['mi:təʳ] The repetition of a pattern of stronger and weaker stresses on the individual syllables of a line or longer passage of verse. In English verse the strong accents generally come at measurable intervals (➧RHYTHM). The basic building-brick of metre is the ➧FOOT.

MIRACLE PLAY ['mɪrakəl pleɪ] A form of religious drama popular from the 12th century to the 15th, mostly representing miracles and other episodes from the lives of the saints. Some authorities on medieval drama use the term 'miracle play' in a wider sense to include events taken from the Bible, or the birth, Passion and death of Christ. ➧ MYSTERY PLAY.

MONOLOGUE ['mɒnəlɒg] In its broadest sense this term denotes any of several kinds of longer speech made by a single character in a play: (1) **Monologue** in the narrower sense: a relatively complete speech of some length, delivered by a single character who is talking to someone (another character [whether present or absent], a personified being, the audience, etc.). This may take the form of a long narrative passage within or at the end of a dialogue scene, or it may be much more independent (forming a distinct part of a scene, or serving as an introduction to a whole play or to one of the acts); (2) **Soliloquy** [sə'lɪləkwi]: an expression of a character's private thoughts and feelings addressed to himself or spoken as if he were alone, though other characters may be present who do not hear what he says. This is a kind of private debate carried out before

17 A. F. Scott, *Current Literary Terms: A Concise Dictionary of their Origin and Use.* London, Melbourne, Toronto: Macmillan 1967, p. 166.
18 W. Nowottny, *The Language Poets Use.* London: The Athlone Press, University of London, 1975 repr. p. 53.

the listening audience; (3) **Aside** [ə'saɪd] (= to the side). Here a character makes a short speech – often in a low voice – in order to express his thoughts, feelings, or intentions. In general an aside is not heard by some or all of the other characters on the stage, for it is meant to be heard only by the audience and sometimes by one or more of the other characters. Like the two other kinds of monologue, asides fulfilled a definite dramatic function in the Elizabethan theatres, in which the stage was surrounded by the audience on at least three sides. ➧ APRON STAGE.

MONOMETER [mə'nɒmɪtər] ➧ FOOT.

MOOD [mu:d] 'A state of the feelings at a particular time'[19]. The **mood** of a literary text may be regarded as 'the emotional or emotional-intellectual attitude which the author takes toward his subject or theme . . . If a distinction is made between **mood** and TONE, it will be the fairly subtle one of **mood** being the emotional attitude of the author toward his subject and TONE the attitude of the author toward his audience.'[20] Also ➧ ATMOSPHERE.

MORALITY PLAY [mə'rælɪtipleɪ] Type of medieval drama of the late 14th, 15th and 16th centuries, designed to teach people and encourage them to avoid sin and to do good. The typical morality play was an ➧ ALLEGORY of the life of man, showing the struggle between personified virtues and vices, or between angels and devils, for the salvation or destruction of the hero, who represents mankind or Everyman. Comic figures like the Vice or the Devil, who played the part of tempters in these plays, have been regarded as among the models of the comic figures (Fools) in Elizabethan plays. Cf. Shakespeare's Hell-porter in MACBETH and the many allegorical figures mentioned in the play: Fortune (I,2,14), Valour (I,2,19), Justice (I,2,29), Chance (I,3,143), etc.

MOTIF [məʊ'ti:f] A single element – a word, phrase, image, object, or action – in a literary text, repeated in order to reproduce a particular association within the mind of the reader or spectator, thus contributing a certain unity to the work as a whole. Example: the idea of 'being a man' or of being 'unmanned' with fear (I,7, 39, 46, 49, 51, 54; III,1, 90, 91, 100, 102, III,4, 58, 59, 73, 99, 106, 108, IV,3, 220, 221, 230, 235; V,2,11; V,9,6; 9).

MYSTERY PLAY ['mɪstəri pleɪ] A type of medieval religious drama, current from the loth to the 15th century, dealing with stories taken from the Old and the New Testament, for example with Christ's birth and Passion, and with his reappearances to his disciples after his death. This type of play, often written In Latin, had its origins in the Christmas, Easter or Whitsun services in the churches, when these religious services began to include short dramatized episodes in about the 10th century. In the course of time these short episodes developed into plays written in the ordinary English of the period, produced by craftsmen and their guilds on platforms outside the churches. By the 14th century these plays or cycles of plays were performed in other places too on the Feast of Corpus Christi. The guildsmen used small moveable stages on wheels, which were known as **pageants** ['pædʒənts] (L pagina = plank). These two-storied wooden structures were rolled through the streets in the proper chronological order of the scenes they showed. On each of these pageants the members of a particular guild performed one scene of the mystery play. As soon as they had finished their scene they moved on to perform it again somewhere else in the town, while the pageant showing the next scene moved forward for a performance of the next of the biblical events. Later on, invented comic scenes were added to these religious plays.

OXYMORON [ˌɒksɪ'mɔ:rɒn] A paradoxical statement that combines contradictory elements of meaning. As they do not agree logically they cannot refer to really existing objects. Example: 'Was the hope drunk,|Wherein you dressed yourself?' (I,7,35f.).

19 P. Procter, ed., et. al., *Dictionary of Contemporary English*. Printed in Great Britain: Langenscheidt-Longman 1978, p. 705: "mood (1)".
20 C. H. Holman, p. 327.

PARADOX ['pærədɒks] A ➧ Rhetorical DEVICE or ➧ FIGURE OF SPEECH in which the speaker or writer expresses a thought whose parts seem to contradict each other at first sight, but do make sense or express some hidden truth when they are considered more deeply on other levels of meaning. The device is a means of expressing and emphasizing complex thoughts by stating them in an apparently absurd way. Example: 'When the battle's lost and won.' (I,1,4).

PARALLELISM ['pærəlelɪzəm] The repetition of patterns of sound and rhythm, of words or larger units of expression, usually linked with variations in other accompanying elements. The kind of parallelism that concerns us in literary criticism is **syntactical** parallelism: the structural arrangement of parts of a sentence, sentences, paragraphs, or larger units of composition in which one element of equal importance with another is expressed in a similar way. This symmetry of clearly-defined and repeated patterns of thought not only helps to stress some important idea, or some similarity between different ideas, it also serves to offset words or phrases against each other, thus establishing a definite contrast. Examples: Contrast: 'This supernatural soliciting |**Cannot be ill; cannot be good:** – **if ill,**|**Why** hath it . . .?|**If good, why** do I yield . . .?' (I,3,130 ff.); expressing a correspondence between two ideas: 'If **chance will have me king,** why, **Chance may crown me,**|Without my stir.' (I,3,144 f.); stressing one main idea: 'I conjure you, . . . **answer me: Though** you untie the winds, . . . **though** the yesty waves|Confound . . .; . . . |**Though** bladed corn be lodged, . . . |**Though** castles topple . . .;|**Though** palaces and pyramids to slope . . . **though** the treasure of nature's germen tumble all together,| . . . **answer me**|To what I ask you' (IV,1,50–61).

PENTAMETER [pen'tæm$^{\text{I}}_{\text{ə}}$təʳ] ➧ FOOT.

PERSONIFICATION [pəˌsɒn$^{\text{I}}_{\text{ə}}$f$^{\text{I}}_{\text{ə}}$'keɪʃən] A ➧ FIGURE OF SPEECH in which lifeless objects or animals, natural events, or abstract ideas are spoken of as if they were human beings. Personification may be regarded as a type of ➧ METAPHOR that gives objects not only life (= animistic metaphor) but also human attributes (= humanizing metaphor). Examples: 'Stars, **hide** your fires!' (I,4,50); 'The raven himself is **hoarse** . . .' (I,5,36 ff.); 'Confusion now **hath made his masterpiece**!' (II,3,62 ff.).

PLOT [plɒt] When used of a play the term **plot** refers to the sequence of events which are arranged not necessarily in a strictly chronological way, but – for the sake of unity and dramatic effect – in a general pattern of cause and effect. The actions of the various characters in the events of the play are part of a conflict between opposing forces. Both these single actions and the conflict itself make up the building material of the plot: they are arranged to form a chain of events which follows the principle of causality.

POETIC JUSTICE [pəʊˌetɪk'dʒʌstɪs] The ideal justice of the playwright, by which virtue is rewarded and vice is punished as a logical consequence of the actions and principles of the characters.

POLYSYNDETON [ˌpɒlɪ'sɪndɪˌtən] **POLYSYNDETIC** [ˌpɒlɪsɪn'detɪk] A ➧ FIGURE OF SPEECH in which more definite or indefinite articles, prepositions or conjunctions than necessary are placed between the separate words or phrases in order to create ➧ EMPHASIS. Example: the grammatically or syntactically unnecessary 'ands' in IV,1,14–17.

PROSE ['prəʊz] Language as it is spoken or written every day for practical purposes. Prose is usually marked by an absence of regular and constantly repeated rhythmic patterns (➧ VERSE). It is used mainly for the exchange of exact information and practical directions, linking ideas and expressing them in a logical and grammatical order. Elizabethan playwrights used prose in purely informative or humorous scenes. Examples: Macbeth's letter (I,5,1–12); the porter's speech (II,3,1 ff.); Lady Macduff's conversation with her son (IV,2,31 f.).

PROTAGONIST [prəʊ'tægənɪ̶st] The main character in a play, the leading figure in the ➧ CONFLICT and the ➧ PLOT. It is he that arouses the greatest amount of interest and sympathy in the spectators. His chief opponent is sometimes called ➧ ANTAGONIST.

PUN [pʌn] A humorous play on words which have either the same or similar sounds but different meanings. Example: 'Come in, tailor, here you may roast your goose' (II,3,12). 'Goose' = (1) a type of large white bird kept on farms, which makes a hissing noise; (2) a flat iron for ironing clothes.

REGISTER ['redʒɪ̶stəʳ] A particular level of language, and especially of vocabulary, suitable for use in a particular kind of social situation. This type of language changes according to subject, speaker, addressee and situation. Example: compare the different registers Lady Macbeth uses when talking to herself (I,5,13ff.), to her husband (I,5,52f.; I,7,35ff.), to King Duncan (I,6,14ff.) and to guests (III,4,53ff.), and to servants (I,5,29ff.).

RELIEF SCENE [rɪ'li:fsi:n] 'A comic scene in a serious play. Its most obvious purpose is to relax the receptor's tension, so as to permit the emotional surge to be later renewed.'[21] Such moments may be provided by ➧ COMIC RELIEF (II,3), or by sentimental dialogue arousing feelings of sorrow and pity (IV,2), or by the protagonist's absence from the stage (IV,3).

RHETORICAL DEVICES [rɪˌtɒrɪkəl dɪ'vaɪsɪz] The second main group of ➧ FIGURES OF SPEECH (after ➧ TROPES). Rhetorical devices (also known as rhetorical figures or rhetorical schemes [ski:mz]) are 'departures from customary or standard uses of language to achieve special effects without a change in the radical meaning of the words'.[22] By their unusual arrangement of words they create effects such as ➧ EMPHASIS without altering the basic meaning of the words themselves (which is what happens with the TROPES). These devices include: ➧ ANAPHORA, ANTITHESIS, APOSTROPHE, ENUMERATION, EXCLAMATION, RHETORICAL QUESTION, HYPERBOLE. Example: King Duncan's hyperbole [haɪ'pɜ:bəli] at I,4,16f.: 'Thou art **so far before,**|That **swiftest wing** of recompense **is slow** to overtake thee'.

RHETORICAL QUESTION [rɪˌtɒrɪkəl'kwestʃən] A ➧ RHETORICAL DEVICE in which a question is asked to which no reply is expected – as the answer is obvious. Often used to persuade people when reasoning with them or inspiring them to carry out some action. Example: 'Who cannot want the thought how monstrous | It was for Malcolm and for Donalbain | to kill their gracious father?' (III,6,8ff.).

RHYME [raɪm] A literary device in which similar sounds are repeated in similar positions, usually at the ends of lines. 'In English versification the standard rhyme consists in the identity, in rhyming words, of the last stressed vowel and of all the speech sounds following that vowel: láte – fáte; fóllow – swállow.'[23] – As to the position of the rhyming syllables in a line there is (1) **End-rhyme**, Example: 'fair – air' (I,1,10/11); and (2) **Internal Rhyme**, in which rhyming occurs somewhere within a line or lines. Example: 'in the great **hand** of God I **stand**; and **thence**|Against the undivulged **pretence** I fight|Of treasonous malice.' (II,3,128–130). – If we classify rhyme according to the number of syllables affected we find two types: (1) **Masculine Rhyme** ['mæskjʊlɪ̶n], which consists of one finally-stressed rhyming syllable, Example: 'done – won – sun' (I,1,3–5); and (2) **Feminine Rhyme** ['femɪ̶nɪ̶n], in which one stressed syllable followed by one unstressed syllable rhymes with a similar pair of syllables. Example: 'illusion – confusion' (III,5,28–29). – Rhyme does not only serve an ornamental function in a literary work. It also serves to structure thoughts and link them into units and to mark the ends of the lines (or the end of a verse paragraph) by a special appeal to the listener's ear. In Shakespearean tragedy end-rhyme is often used to mark the end of a scene.

21 J. T. Shipley, p. 71.
22 C. H. Holman, p. 224.
23 M. H. Abrams, p. 150.

EYE RHYME is what happens with pairs of words whose spelling suggests that they rhyme, but which do not in fact do so. Example: 'are – dare' (III,4,2–3).

RHYME SCHEME ['raɪm,ski:m] The pattern of arrangement of rhyme sounds in the lines of a poem, etc. Students of literature generally use the letters of the alphabet to identify the various possible rhyme schemes. Here are some of the possibilities of a four-line stanza with two different rhymes: (1) **rhyme pairs** (= couplets ['kʌplᵊts]): aabb; (2) **alternating rhyme** [,ɔ:ltəneɪtɪŋ 'raɪm]: abab; (3) **enclosed rhyme:** abba.

RHYMING JINGLE [,raɪmɪŋ 'dʒɪŋgəl] A rather unusual or too noticeable arrangement of identical or similar sounds with alliteration, repetition, rhyme, etc. Such 'jingles' attract our attention because of their unusual effects, which may remind us of the ringing noise made by small bells or pieces of metal like keys or coins. Example: 'hurlyburly' (I,1,3).

RHYTHM ['rɪðəm] in verse this is the passage of regular and almost equal periods of time between the accents on the stressed syllables, within a repeated pattern of stressed and unstressed syllables (➧METRE). In both ➧ PROSE and ➧ VERSE 'the presence of rhythmic patterns lends both pleasure and heightened emotional response to the listener or reader, for it establishes for him a pattern of expectations and rewards him with the pleasure of a series of fulfilments or gratifications of expectation.'[24] Rhythm may be **rising** if each ➧ FOOT begins with an unstressed syllable or syllables and ends with a stressed syllable or syllables; e.g. the ➧ IAMB and the ➧ ANAPAEST. In **falling** rhythm the feet begin with stressed and end with unstressed syllables; e.g. the ➧ DACTYL and the ➧ TROCHEE.

RISING ACTION One of the structural elements of the ➧ PLOT of a tragedy. It comes after the ➧ EXPOSITION, is introduced by the ➧ EXCITING FORCE and includes the various stages of ➧ CONFLICT which mark the advance of the protagonist's fortunes till the turning-point or ➧ CLIMAX is reached and the ➧ FALLING ACTION begins.

RUN-ON LINE ➧ ENJAMBEMENT.

SARCASM ['sa:kæzəm] Remarks that clearly mean the opposite of what is really felt. They often contain a strong element of personal disapproval. Example: Lenox's comments on Macbeth's reactions to the murder of the king: 'How it **did grieve** Macbeth! did he not **straight,**|In **pious rage,** the two **delinquents** tear,|That were the **slaves of drink** and **thralls of sleep**?|Was that not **nobly** done?' etc. (III,6,11 ff.).

SCHEME]ski:m] ➧ RHETORICAL DEVICES.

SETTING ['setɪŋ] 'The setting of a narrative or dramatic work is the general locale and the historical time in which its action occurs; the setting of an episode or scene within a work is the particular physical location in which it takes place. The general setting of MACBETH, for example, is medieval Scotland, and the setting for the scene in which Macbeth comes upon the witches is a blasted heath'.[25]

SIMILE ['sɪmᵊli] A ➧ FIGURE OF SPEECH, one of the four main types of ➧ TROPE. This device expresses a similarity between two objects by making a clearly-stated comparison between them through the use of such constructions as 'like', 'as . . . as', 'not as . . . as'. The object so compared is known as the ➧ TENOR and the object with which it is being compared is known as the ➧ VEHICLE. What the two compared objects have in common may also be expressed. This is known as the ➧ GROUND. Example: (I,2,16–19) 'brave Macbeth . . . (= Tenor) Like Valour's minion . . .'

24 C. H. Holman, p. 456.
25 M. H. Abrams, p. 157.

(= Vehicle); in this case the Ground has to be worked out.[26] It is probably 'out-standing and proverbial bravery'.

SOLILOQUY [sə'lɪləkwi] ➧ MONOLOGUE

STAGE DIRECTIONS ['steɪdʒ dɪ̆ˌrekʃənz] The printed or handwritten information and instructions provided by the author for the producer, actors, or readers of a play, giving important details about the setting, characters, and action or the positions, movements, disguises, gestures, reactions, etc. of the actors impersonating the characters. In this way the actors are advised how to perform the play, while the reader is helped to imagine details he cannot get from the dialogue and action of the play.

SUSPENSE [sə'spens] 'A state of uncertain expectation'.[27] In the case of a play the author makes us feel this kind of excited uncertainty, partly enjoyable and partly painful, about the result of the plot, and especially about its effect upon a particular character or characters to whom we have become bound by feelings of affection, respect or sympathy.

SWEAR WORD ['sweəwɜːd] A taboo word used more or less thoughtlessly to express anger, hatred, etc. Such words form a linguistic register which is socially shocking because of improper use of religious words. Many swear words were originally curses, used to ask God to bring down evil or punishment and destruction on someone or something. Example: 'damned fact!' (III,6,10).

SYMBOL ['sɪmbəl] In the widest sense a symbol is anything meaning or representing sth. else. Thus if two friends or lovers are parting for a time and break a gold ring in two, each keeping one half, the two pieces not only serve as a sign of recognition but also express the unity of their minds and hearts: like the two halves of the ring the lovers are 'made for each other'. In literature a symbol is a kind of ➧TROPE. To some extent a symbol is like an image, for both call up in our minds a picture of a real object or concrete action which we can almost see, hear, touch, taste, or smell. But unlike an image a symbol not only calls up the object and the ordinary meanings connected with it but also makes it represent things or ideas not normally connected with it. Thus a symbol makes us imagine an object which in its turn directs our minds to a level of ideas beyond itself, that is, outside the scope of its usual meanings. There are many conventional symbols whose meaning everbody agrees upon (cross, heart, etc.), and there are also the symbols poets create or enrich; objects, etc. that are given symbolic significance by associations and ideas built up within particular works of art. Example: the bell that is heard at the end of Macbeth's soliloquy (II,1,61) is not only a metallic vessel producing a ringing sound, it is also the pre-arranged signal for him to commit his crime. Thus this bell may be regarded as symbolizing Duncan's death: it is tolling (a little in advance) for him and his passage into the after-life.

TENOR ['tenəʳ] The general idea or literal subject of a ➧METAPHOR or ➧SIMILE, the thing or idea which is compared to or illustrated by the ➧VEHICLE. Also ➧ANALOGY, ➧GROUND, ➧ METAPHOR. Example: 'my gashes (= Tenor) cry for help' (I,2,43). Vehicle: 'cry for help' like open mouths.

TETRAMETER [te'træmɪ̆təʳ] ➧FOOT.

THEME [θiːm] In the case of non-fictional works this is usually the subject or general topic. In a work of imaginative literature the theme is the chief idea or set of ideas that has a controlling influence upon the work as a whole.

TONE [təʊn] The apparent attitude shown by an author towards his listeners or readers in a particular work (e.g. ironical, solemn, informal, etc.). Together with ➧ MOOD (= the author's

26 G. N. Leech, *A Linguistic Guide to English Poetry.* London: Longman, 1971, repr. p. 153ff.
27 P. Procter, ed., et al., p. 1121: "suspense".

feelings about his subject or theme) tone creates the ➧ ATMOSPHERE of a particular fictional world.

TRAGEDY ['trædʒɪdi] A thoughtful and solemn prose or verse drama representing important and serious actions or events in the ➧ PROTAGONIST'S life which are linked by cause and effect and lead to his final overthrow, failure, ruin, and usually also his death. At different periods the elements of tragedy have been interpreted differently in accordance with changing social attitudes and philosophical ideas. Thus in earlier periods the tragic hero was generally a person of high social position, whereas in our own day he is often a quite ordinary person. At about the time of Shakespeare tragedy began to be influenced by the so-called ➧ UNITIES which were believed to have been laid down by Aristotle: the unities of action, time, and place. – People's ideas of what may be considered 'tragic' have also changed over the centuries: e.g. a man's hubris and downfall, or his being confronted with an impossible choice between two alternatives, or his realization that his life has become meaningless. Though Aristotle's definition of tragedy cannot be adapted to all the changing concepts of tragedy that have developed since his day his idea that it should imitate a single action in a serious and complete manner led to the important concept of the unity of action as a source of ➧ PLOT. Aristotle points out that the events in a tragedy create pity and fear but also cleanse ['klenz] the emotions of the spectators (= catharsis [kə'θa:sɪs]): the pity and fear relieve any private pain or trouble in their minds and encourage cheerful or holy feelings despite the fact that they are watching a drama of failure and suffering. No matter how the pleasurable and emotionally cleansing effects of tragedy are explained, Aristotle's concept of catharsis remains an important means by which we can distinguish tragedy from other forms of drama.

TRAGIC FORCE ['trædʒɪk 'fɔ:s] In a tragedy, the situation or influence causing the beginning of the protagonist's misfortunes (➧ FALLING ACTION) and leading to his finale downfall (➧ CATASTROPHE). In MACBETH it is identical with the turning-point or ➧ CRISIS of the hero's fortunes (III,3,17), which goes by without being fully recognized as such by the audience – for the more striking ➧ CLIMAX which follows it in III,4 has a greater emotional impact. Also ➧ EXCITING FORCE, RISING ACTION, DRAMATIC STRUCTURE OF TRAGEDY.

TRIPLET ['trɪplɪt] A three-line stanza, held together by a single rhyme. The three lines may be of identical or different length and consist of the same or different kinds of ➧ FOOT. Example: The first words of the 2nd and 3rd witches at I,1,3–5, taken together, make up a triplet.

TRANSFERRED EPITHET [træns'fɜ:d 'epɪθet] ➧ EPITHET, ➧ EMPHASIS.

TROCHEE ['trəʊki] **TROCHAIC** [trəʊ'keɪ-ɪk] A verse ➧ FOOT consisting of one stressed syllable followed by one unstressed syllable. Example (of a pair of trochees): '**w**orthy **B**anquo (I,4,54).

TROPE [trəʊp] Tropes are a group of ➧ FIGURES OF SPEECH in which words are used in such a manner that their literal or basic meaning is altered. There are four main types of trope: ➧ SIMILE, ➧ METAPHOR, ➧ IMAGE, and ➧ SYMBOL.

UNITIES The unities were a set of three rules for dramatic writing, designed to encourage playwrights to produce well-ordered, integrated works of art. These rules called for unity of action, time and place. It was in 16th-century Italy and 17th-century France that the unities were based more or less on Aristotle's observations on tragedy in the **Poetics.** His statement that the action of a tragedy should be complete, with a beginning, a middle, and an end, and that its parts should be linked together by causality created the important principle of **unity of action** (➧ PLOT). As Aristotle could naturally only study the limited dramatic material of his own day he noted that tragedies tried to limit their action to roughly a single revolution of the sun. This was the origin of the 16th- and 17th-century concept of the **unity of time.** Thus Italian critics in the late Renaissance claimed that the tragic action should be limited to one day, a rule that was quite strictly followed by the French classical dramatists of the 17th century. – Although Aristotle did not mention the **unity of place** according to which the dramatic action was to be confined to a single location (the same room, or house, or city) Italian critics laid it down as a rule because of the limitation of the dramatic events to a period of a few hours. For the sake of realism the acting time of a play on the stage had to correspond to the period of time occupied by its plot. – In his tragedies Shakespeare more or less followed the unity of action, but almost completely disregarded the unities of time and place. Instead he followed another principle of unity which may be called **unity of tone and atmosphere.**

VEHICLE ['viːɪkəl] In a ➧ METAPHOR or ➧ SIMILE, whatever the subject is compared to. The vehicle serves to concentrate attention on the subject by illustrating it. Example: 'Life's but a walking shadow' (V,5,24). Here 'life' is the tenor or subject of the metaphor, and 'walking shadow' is the object or vehicle. The ➧ GROUND (whatever it is that tenor and vehicle have in common) has to be worked out by the reader or listener: it is transience, lack of any substance, restless movement, etc.

VERBAL IRONY [ˌvɜːbəl 'aɪərəni] A ➧ FIGURE OF SPEECH which, unlike ➧ DRAMATIC IRONY, is addressed to one audience only. This audience is expected to understand not only the fully expressed and pretended meaning of the statement but also, at the same time, the opposite and really intended meaning carried by the words. Irony is less hurtful than ➧ SARCASM but can be a clever and effective instrument despite (or because of) its indirectness. Example: 'Are you so **gospelled**|To **pray** for this **good** man, and for his issue,|Whose heavy hand hath bowed you to the grave|And beggared yours for ever? (III,1,87).

VERSE [vɜːs] Writing arranged in more or less regular lines, with a more or less definite rhythm and sometimes with ➧ RHYMES at the ends of the lines; the opposite of ➧ PROSE.

VERSE DRAMA ['vɜːsˌdraːmə] or ['–'– –] or [ˌ–'– –] Sometimes called 'poetic drama'. A play written wholly or mainly in verse, usually ➧ BLANK VERSE. The lines have a more or less regular rhythmic patterning, and in Shakespeare's plays there are occasional rhyming lines (at the ends of scenes, etc.). Shakespeare's plays are poetic dramas.

Acknowledgements

We are grateful to the following for permission to reproduce copyright material and photographs:

Texts:

Verlag Lambert Schneider, Heidelberg for p. 108; W. Krieg Verlag, Wien for p. 108; Albert Langen-Georg Müller Verlag, München for p. 109;

Illustrations:

ZERO – angewandte Grafik, München, for p. 12; Oxford University Press for p. 13 and 16, taken from: Sir E. K. Chambers, *William Shakespeare: A Study of Facts and Problems,* Oxford: Clarendon Press 1963; The Shakespeare Birthplace Trust, Stratford-upon-Avon, for p. 13; Cambridge University Press for p. 17, taken from: Andrew Gurr, *The Elizabethan Stage 1574–1642,* Cambridge 1970; p. 18, taken from: D. Wilson, *Life in Shakespeare's England.* Cambridge 1951; The Trustees of the National Library of Scotland, Edinburgh, for p. 23; G. G. Harrap Ltd., London, for p. 26, taken from: Allardyce Nicoll, *British Drama: An Historical Survey from the Beginnings to the Present Time.* London 1953, repr.; Penguin Books Ltd. for p. 27, taken from: G. B. Harrison, *Introducing Shakespeare.* Harmondsworth: Pelican Books Ltd. 3rd rev. ed. 1966; Royal Commission on Historical Monuments (England), London, for p. 28; Granada Publishing Ltd.; St. Albans, for p. 30 and p. 35, taken from: L. Hotson, *Shakespeare's Wooden O.* London: Rupert Hart-Davis 1960; The Folger Shakespeare Library, Washington, for p. 39; Harvard College Library for p. 40, taken from: G. Blakemore Evans, textual ed. et. al., *The Riverside Shakespeare.* Boston: Houghton Mifflin Company 1974; Penguin Books Ltd. for p. 51, taken from: J. J. Bayley and P. B. Rowley, *A Documentary History of England, Vol. I: 1066–1540.* Harmondsworth 1968, repr.; Bilderdienst Süddeutscher Verlag for pp. 46, 47, 48, 52, 57, 58, 60; Columbia Pictures, New York, for cover photo and all photos in "Part II: Background Reading", taken from the film *Great Themes of Literature* (= a shortened version of Polanski's film MACBETH, published by Institut für Film und Bild in Wissenschaft und Unterricht, München).